Schoolyard-Enhanced Learning

Schoolyard-Enhanced Learning
Using the Outdoors as an Instructional Tool, K–8

Herbert W. Broda

Stenhouse Publishers
Portland, Maine

Stenhouse Publishers
www.stenhouse.com

Library of Congress Cataloging-in-Publication Data

Broda, Herbert W., 1945-
  Schoolyard-enhanced learning : using the outdoors as an instructional tool, K–8 / Herbert W. Broda.
      p. cm.
  Includes bibliographical references and index.
  ISBN 978-1-57110-729-9 (alk. paper)
  1. Outdoor education. I. Title.
  LB1047.B76 2007
  372.13'84--dc22
                                  2007025980

Photo Credits:
Emily Baxter: back cover
Boston Schoolyard Funders Collaborative: 2.2a, 2.2b, 2.4, 2.5, and 2.6
Janet Broda: 4.2a and 4.2b
Matthew Broda: front cover, 5.1, 5.2a, and 5.2b
Laura Grimm: 4.3
All other photos are by the author.

Cover design, interior design, and typesetting by: Designboy Creative Group
Manufactured in the United States of America on acid-free, recycled paper
13 12 11 10 09   9 8 7 6 5 4 3 2

To my wife, Janet, and our children, Emily, Matthew, and Michael.
Sharing nature with you is my idea of a perfect day.

Contents

Acknowledgments

I thought that writing the acknowledgments would be easy! Easy it was not. This book builds upon decades of experiences, as well as a philosophy that has been shaped and rethought through school visits, readings, and countless conversations with students, teachers, and colleagues. It's impossible to identify all of the influences that are reflected in these pages, but I want to highlight a few.

I am greatly indebted to several people whom I interviewed during my research. Their candid and enthusiastic responses reaffirmed my commitment to outdoor learning and provided practical, teacher-tested advice and activities. A special thank you to these folks:

Kristin Metz and Kirk Meyer of the Boston Schoolyard Initiative (BSI) provided practical suggestions and wonderful photos. I was delighted to discover this organization that is dedicated to promoting the enhancement and use of the schoolyard for instruction. The good that BSI is doing in the Boston area is both amazing and inspiring.

Teacher Linda Lang, an avid birder, shared her enthusiasm and insights for integrating the outdoors into instruction. Her experience enhancing the school grounds for outdoor instruction at two elementary schools provided many practical tips. I enjoyed an interview in a camp dining hall with longtime camp director Jerry Dunlap and his son, Trevor. They shared their philosophy and approach to initiative tasks and spoke eloquently of the power of a camp experience. Their enthusiasm is infectious.

There are three additional teachers who not only were interviewed, but also supplied student work samples, site visit opportunities, photos, print materials, and most important, constant encouragement for this project: Sue Cook and I have worked together for decades, collaborating on dozens of outdoor-education workshops and courses. Sue was probably the first teacher I ever knew who approached the use of the outdoors as a teaching tool with almost missionary zeal. Her enthusiasm for the concept has been an inspiration to me.

Laura Grimm's creativity, practical insights, and great outdoor learning activities are referred to throughout this book. I have learned much from my many visits to Laura's school and the outdoor learning area that she was instrumental in creating.

Although Josh Flory is a relatively new teacher, he quickly saw the value and impact of schoolyard-enhanced learning for middle school students. He is always designing new outdoor learning projects and has provided support to this project in dozens of ways.

I need to acknowledge my inquiry seminar graduate students who, over the years, have shared their ideas and fueled my enthusiasm for outdoor learning. They have reaffirmed for me that outdoor learning is not unique to any specific grade level or content area.

Over the years, I have been blessed with wonderful work environments that supported and encouraged my interest in outdoor learning. The Southeast Local School District, Tri-County Educational Service Center, and Ashland University all have been helpful in unique and meaningful ways.

Thank you also to Bill Varner, senior editor at Stenhouse. Bill has patiently worked with this first-timer from the proposal stage all the way to publication. His insight, creativity, and professionalism have truly shaped this book. Thanks also to Erin Trainer and Jay Kilburn at Stenhouse for their creativity and enthusiasm as the book moved into production.

I have been blessed with a wonderfully loving and supportive family. My wife, Janet, has been always understanding and always patient as this seemingly endless process of "writing the book" has unfolded. I owe a huge debt to our three children, Emily, Matthew, and Michael, who, during their childhoods, often served as field testers of new activities and unexplored trails, only occasionally muttering, "Are we going to The Wilderness Center *again*?" This awesome family has constantly nurtured my sense of wonder.

Chapter 1

Schoolyard-Enhanced Learning: A Change of Pace and Place

It's amazing how a casual comment can sometimes impact our actions and feelings for years. As a new and enthusiastic sixth-grade teacher, I was bringing my students back to the classroom after doing a math lesson outdoors. I passed a colleague in the hall who stopped, smiled, and said, "Must be nice to go outside and play instead of teach."

Although the comment was just lighthearted kidding, I still couldn't help feeling annoyed and even a bit uncomfortable. I was annoyed that my colleague obviously defined "real" teaching as something that could take place only inside a classroom. But I was a new teacher, and the remark also raised the uncomfortable notion that maybe I wasn't making the best use of time. After years of reflection and experience, though, I am more convinced than ever that the best use of time occurs when kids are actively engaged in motivating learning activities and environments, either indoors or beyond the walls of the classroom.

Looking at the comment from the vantage point of the twenty-first century, I feel confident that, today, a very different mind-set exists concerning alternative venues for learning. Of course, there are many who still contend that "real" learning must be unpleasant, abstract, and defined exclusively by four walls. Thankfully, however, many

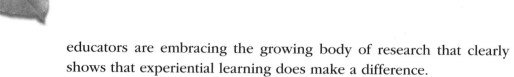

educators are embracing the growing body of research that clearly shows that experiential learning does make a difference.

Moving Beyond the Four Walls

Confining learning exclusively to the four walls of a classroom just doesn't make sense. Increased academic achievement and heightened enthusiasm for learning, coupled with decreased discipline problems, all have been associated with learning that happens beyond the school walls. The concepts of learning style and multiple intelligences are also very compatible with outdoor learning activities. Frankly, outdoor learning would be a logical addition to our instructional repertoire simply because it adds interest and variety to our teaching—a change of pace and place.

It's impossible to say who "discovered" outdoor instruction. Indeed, it's probable that observant teachers throughout history have noted that children learn best when they have firsthand experience with their environment.

Friedrich Froebel, often cited as the originator of the "kindergarten system" in the nineteenth century, was a strong believer in the value of play and active learning. A major premise of his theory was that understanding follows concrete experience. Froebel also was one of the first to develop special objects and materials (today we might call them manipulatives) to use as instructional tools. His concept of kindergarten encouraged frequent contact with nature as a part of the learning experience.

During the late 1800s and early 1900s, the heavy industrialization of the United States precipitated an interest in looking beyond the smokestacks and factories to the natural world. The nature study movement espoused the intriguing idea that children were innately interested in nature and were "born naturalists." The nature study movement saw nature as a teaching tool. Proponents urged teachers to leave the classroom and take students outside for direct experience.

Historian Kevin Armitage notes that, although nature was viewed as an excellent vehicle for teaching science, nature study enthusiasts also saw the outdoors as an innovation for teaching a variety of concepts, in areas from from critical investigation to spiritual, literary, and aesthetic knowledge.

Nature study teachers felt that direct contact with the natural world—getting kids out of the classroom and into woods, fields and streams—would reconcile the disparate goals of promoting scientific and spiritual relationships with nature. (2007)

The outdoors was emerging not only as a source of content but also as a teaching tool.

We Need More "Wows" and "Ahas"

"If a child is to keep alive his inborn sense of wonder, he needs the companionship of at least one adult who can share it, rediscovering with him the joy, excitement and mystery of the world we live in."

—Rachel Carson

Although there are many good reasons for taking students outside—educational, social, aesthetic, recreational—I have to admit that one of my most compelling reasons is to provide opportunities for kids to experience that sense of wonder that Rachel Carson talked about. It always happens in very unexpected and totally unplanned ways—a child discovers the iridescent wings of a dragonfly, the intricacy of a spiderweb, or the smell of freshly spaded earth. I like to think that an accumulation of those "aha" experiences results in both a sense of wonder and subsequent feelings of responsibility and stewardship. The more we take children outside for learning activities, the greater the probability for moments of awe and insight.

But in today's world, it's getting harder and harder to hear the "ahas." The recent popularity of Richard Louv's book, *Last Child in the Woods: Saving Our Children from Nature-Deficit Disorder*, has encouraged an important dialogue about the role of nature in our lives. Louv directly addresses our growing estrangement with the natural world from several angles. A significant part of the problem is related to our addiction to technological gadgetry.

An Ocean of Media

Gregory Lamb writes of the "media ecosystem" that is surrounding us. In his words, we are swimming in an "ocean of media" (2005, 13). We have PDAs, MP3 players, handheld computers, and phones that can do practically everything electronically!

3

Of course, neither television nor the Internet is "bad." Like all media, they can facilitate both life-enhancing as well as mind-numbing experiences. My concern is that entire households have become so caught up in technogadgetry that outdoor leisure activities are viewed less and less as viable options.

As individuals, we need to examine our own priorities of pace and place. Too often we have chosen to be plugged in, but tuned out. The place is often in front of a screen, and the pace is usually hectic.

Ironically, another factor that keeps kids isolated from nature is our obsession with providing our children with experiences—as many as possible. It's still a little disconcerting to me to see a fourth grader checking an appointment book! As a society, we are blessed (I think!) with a record number of highly organized recreational, sports, hobby, and arts activities. For some reason, though, we seem to feel that our children need to participate in as many of these organized experiences as possible. The result is rather predictable; when you combine very busy kids' schedules with stressed and overworked parents' schedules, there usually is not much room for leisurely outdoor activity or exploration.

Many kids wouldn't even consider the outdoors as a place to spend the half hour before dinner. Why bother? The lure of interactive technology is too tempting. And "dinner" may just be a trip through a drive-thru on the way to yet another lesson, game, or practice.

Fifth-grade teacher Linda Lang has a great way to solve the problem: "Let kids just dig in the dirt. Let them get dirty and take a look at what's in the soil. So many kids have never done that."

She is so right. Many kids simply have not had the opportunity to explore outside. Linda refers to the "wow" factor—that excitement that develops when video-saturated kids see something unexpected in nature.

Whether you call it a "sense of wonder" or the "wow" factor, it's a response that is innate for all of us. I'm fascinated to watch my two-year-old grandson interact with his own backyard. Stones are reverently turned in little hands, flowers are gently sniffed, and even tiny insects are blessed with wide-eyed curiosity, as can be seen in Figure 1.1.

All too often, however, many kids have this natural sense of wonder quickly eclipsed by flat-panel screens and busy schedules. Digging in the dirt is replaced by staring at video images, and unstructured play time is trumped by an overstocked appointment calendar. For many students, school may be the only place where they are encouraged to interact with nature.

Figure 1.1 Curiosity and exploration generate a sense of wonder about the natural world.

What Is Outdoor Education?

The Name Game

For nearly a century, the general phrase "outdoor education" has been used for learning activities that take place outside—at a camp, on the school grounds, or in the community. Because "outdoor education" has been around for such a long time, it has morphed into a variety of meanings. One outdoor education website, www.wilderdom.com lists more than fifty terms that are described as similar to or closely related to outdoor education (Neill).

It's certainly encouraging that the concept is constantly evolving, but the multiple definitions that have arisen can be confusing. I'm always fascinated how the term *outdoor education* is associated with so many different experiences. Whenever I mention my interest in outdoor education, I get a wide variety of enthusiastic responses, including:

"My school goes to camp each year."

"My daughter took an Outward Bound course."

"Our sixth grade has a recycling program."

"I took my students outside for language arts."

"We have a ropes course in our community."

"My son learned how to fish this summer."

Outdoor education seems to include everything from camping to environmental problem-solving to writing a poem under a tree on the playground! Perhaps the reason why it's difficult to precisely label "outdoor education" is because it really isn't a technical term. Rather, "outdoor education" refers to a general concept—the idea

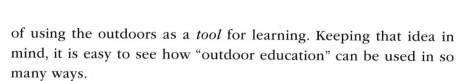

of using the outdoors as a *tool* for learning. Keeping that idea in mind, it is easy to see how "outdoor education" can be used in so many ways.

Outdoor education is really a subset of the more general concept of experiential learning. The major elements of experiential learning—using authentic experiences and learning by doing—are also integral parts of outdoor teaching. For example, to visualize the concept of "camouflage," one teacher has pairs of students cut out moth shapes from birthday wrapping paper and glue them onto another sheet of paper with the same pattern. With just a quick look, other pairs have to count how many "moths" they see. A discussion follows as to why the moths were so difficult to find. Another teacher reinforces the concept of camouflage by taking kids outside to cut out paper snakes and color them so that they blend in with a garden on the school grounds. In both cases elements of experiential learning have been used.

Experiential learning refers to a process and is not limited to a specific venue. Students conducting experiments or simulations in a classroom are engaging in experiential learning. The setting of the experience isn't the defining element since students are observing and reflecting upon concrete experiences in order to clarify or formulate abstract concepts. Outdoor education, however, specifically refers to experiences that take place outside. The observation, reflection, and concept clarification occur outdoors.

Three Dimensions of Outdoor Education

Historically, the outdoor education concept has been used to refer to three broad categories of learning. These multiple interpretations make it difficult to construct a single "definition" for the term, although the common thread in each case is that students are going outside for the activity or experience. Over the years, schools have used the outdoors to:

- promote both a knowledge of and a concern for the environment.
- facilitate personal growth through problem-solving, challenge, and adventure.
- focus upon the teaching of traditional subject matter.

Promote Knowledge of and Concern for the Environment

Environmental Education

For many years, the term *conservation education* was also referred to as outdoor education. Strong emphasis was placed upon a stewardship ethic and the wise use of natural resources. Gradually, the concept of conservation education morphed into the broader concept of environmental education.

By the early 1980s, the term *environmental education* was in general use and eclipsed the term *conservation education*. People began to include conservation education and traditional outdoor learning practices under the title "environmental education." In Ohio, for example, the long-established Ohio Conservation and Outdoor Education Association changed its name to the Environmental Education Council of Ohio.

The early environmental education movement has been international in scope. Two major documents are usually cited as driving forces behind the formal emergence of "environmental education." The Belgrade Charter (1976) and the Tbilisi Declaration (1978) were both supported by the United Nations Educational, Scientific and Cultural Organization— United Nations Environment Programme (UNESCO-UNEP). The Belgrade Charter articulated a goal for environmental education:

> *The goal of environmental education is to develop a world population that is aware of, and concerned about, the environment and its associated problems, and which has the knowledge, skills, attitudes, motivations, and commitment to work individually and collectively toward solutions of current problems and the prevention of new ones. (United Nations Educational 1975, 3)*

This goal statement provided a framework for the world's first intergovernmental conference on environmental education, which then adopted the Tbilisi Declaration. Adkins and Simmons state that the declaration

> *suggests that the basic aim of environmental education is to help individuals and communities understand the complex nature of the natural and built environments resulting from the interaction of their biological, physical, social, economic and cultural aspects, and acquire the knowledge, values, attitudes and practical skills to participate in a responsible and effective way in solving environmental problems, and in the management of the quality of the environment. (2003, 3)*

7

Environmental education was evolving with two major areas of focus:

1) the study of the complexity and interactions of the natural and built environments

2) a strong commitment to developing the knowledge, skills, attitudes, and values needed to produce an informed citizenry that could work to identify and solve environmental problems

Programs today that use the label "environmental education" contain these two dimensions, although the degree of emphasis upon each element can vary greatly. Some programs primarily emphasize the understanding of ecological concepts, while others focus heavily upon issues, problems, and strategies for improving the environment.

Environment-Based Education

Although environmental education is still being utilized in a wide variety of forms, the term *environment-based education* (EBE) is appearing frequently in the literature. According to the National Environmental Education and Training Foundation, environment-based education has the following characteristics:

- Integrated learning across disciplines
- Problem-solving
- Decision-making
- Independent and group learning
- Issues-based instructional activities
- A balanced variety of perspectives

(2000, 12)

These characteristics are woven together by using the environment as the focal point or primary organizer. The idea is similar to the concept of interdisciplinary units that are organized around broad themes or topics. A companion concept that is frequently cited is the use of the environment as an integrating context, often referred to as EIC (State Education and Environment Roundtable 2006).

Place-Based Education

The relatively new term *place-based education* is also very compatible with the concept of using the outdoors for learning. Place-based education encourages teachers to move beyond the school walls to create learning experiences that are centered on the school grounds and in the broader community. The local community is emphasized as the focal point of learning experiences and is used to teach traditional subject matter concepts.

Place-based education also shares its roots with environmental education. Although place-based education is certainly not synonymous with environmental education, there are strong connections. Educational researcher Amy Powers states that "Place-based education has emerged from a thirty-year foundation of environmental education in the United States and builds on the work of diverse community-based initiatives" (2004, 17).

David Sobel articulates the view that "Place-based education takes us back to basics, but in a broader and more inclusive fashion . . . The history, folk culture, social problems, and the aesthetics of the community are all on the agenda" (2004, 9). Good place-based programs incorporate many of the environment-based education elements listed above, and use the community as the integrating context and teaching resource.

Doing Research to Nurture Responsibility

It was an odd parade—a string of twenty high school students making their way along a narrow trail that led to the stream. Everyone was carrying something—either waders, nets, GPS devices, clipboards, or water-testing kits. Once at the stream bank, everyone had a job. Pairs of students were stationed at varying distances along (and in!) the stream. Information was carefully recorded for analysis back in the classroom. Data from this field experience would then be compared with information from four prior years of analysis at the same site.

The real learning came as students used the data to form hypotheses about the quality of the stream over time. Discussion quickly moved to speculation concerning the impact of new housing units that had been built upstream. This class was embracing both dimensions of environmental education: the interactions of natural and built environments were being researched, and a sense of environmental responsibility was being encouraged.

9

Facilitate Personal Growth Through Problem-Solving, Challenge, and Adventure

Of the three dimensions of outdoor learning, personal growth through problem-solving, challenge, and adventure is probably the most difficult to do in the schoolyard. Some high schools have ropes courses or challenge course equipment on site, but the equipment cost and need for specialized training make it prohibitive for most. Camps or outdoor learning centers with the needed equipment are frequently within a reasonable drive and are usually eager to conduct sessions for school groups.

Schools can, however, use the schoolyard effectively to develop problem-solving skills, trust, and leadership. Initiative tasks are problem situations that are explained by a leader/teacher and require a group to work together to demonstrate a solution. These tasks often can be done either indoors or out, but many initiatives use props and equipment that are best utilized outdoors.

Initiatives are often used to build a sense of community and camaraderie in a group. The three main elements of an initiative activity are:

1) explanation of the problem situation
2) group discussion and problem-solving attempts
3) debriefing of the experience

Most initiative task leaders feel that the debriefing component, in which participants analyze the group dynamics that occurred, is the most defining aspect of an initiative task experience. Chapter 6 provides a more detailed discussion of the initiative task concept, including specific ways to debrief any group problem-solving activity.

A problem-solving activity may be as simple as having a group stand on a piece of tarp and figure out how to turn it over without anyone ever touching the ground. Or, it could be a practical experience in which students problem-solve the best locations for five bird feeders on the school grounds.

Schools that provide resident outdoor-education (school camping) programs often take advantage of the unique camp setting and include initiative/challenge activities in the curriculum. These may range from simple on-the-ground challenges to more elaborate rope elements.

The resident camp experience, even without formally planned initiative task experiences, can foster the development of social skills and a sense of independence. For a twelve-year-old, spending a few nights in a cabin can be a real source of challenge and adventure.

The term *outdoor education* is also frequently used to refer to programs that usually occur outside of a school setting and provide opportunities for individuals to focus on various dimensions of personal growth through challenging or out-of-the-ordinary experiences. Two examples of familiar national programs include Outward Bound and the National Outdoor Leadership School (NOLS). These programs were launched in the United States during the 1960s and 1970s, and are still popular. Today, there are literally thousands of programs offered by a multitude of agencies, organizations, and institutions that take individuals outside to help them grow as persons.

An abundance of programs also are targeted for youth and adults with special needs. These frequently are overnight or day camp experiences and have been used for dropout prevention programs, substance abuse prevention, and a variety of other physical and mental health concerns. Indeed, entire academic concentrations exist in such areas as adventure and wilderness therapy, recreation therapy, and outdoor behavioral health care. These types of outdoor programs clearly are intended to facilitate personal growth through challenge and adventure.

Richard Louv makes a strong case for the personal growth that can occur in nature:

> *Nature—the sublime, the harsh, the beautiful—offers something that the street or gated community or computer game cannot. Nature presents the young with something so much greater than they are; it offers an environment where they can easily contemplate infinity and eternity. (2005, 97)*

Although not as dramatic as ropes courses or overnight camping, just spending time outdoors on the school grounds can most certainly facilitate personal growth.

Teach Traditional Subject Matter

The primary focus of this book is to emphasize this third dimension of outdoor education: ways to use the outdoors as a learning tool to teach traditional subjects in the school curriculum. Julian Smith, a Michigan State University professor and a highly influential promoter of outdoor learning during the mid-twentieth century, saw outdoor education as a means of curriculum enrichment. He referred to it as a learning climate that offered the opportunity for direct experiences (Smith et al. 1970, 20). Outdoor education is not a subject area; rather it is an instructional tool that can be used to enhance instruction in a variety of disciplines.

Too often, the concept of outdoor learning is equated only with teaching science. The sciences are certainly well suited to outdoor instruction, but other content areas can benefit from moving beyond the classroom walls as well. Language arts, mathematics, social studies, creative writing, the arts, physical education—all can benefit from the change of pace and place that comes with outdoor instruction.

The Natural Difference

Four words were defined on the chalkboard with a few examples under each: adjective, adverb, simile, and metaphor. After defining descriptive writing and reviewing the terms, the teacher asked the class to write a paragraph describing something in nature. The results showed a basic understanding of the terms, but certainly couldn't be called striking examples of vivid description.

At the start of class the next day, the teacher took the group outside and repeated the assignment that everyone should write a paragraph describing something in nature. The results were impressive. Although the subject was the same, students used a completely different vocabulary to describe what they actually saw. The outdoors had become a vehicle for teaching traditional subject matter.

Although outdoor instruction is a powerful teaching strategy, I want to be clear that I am not advocating that all or even most traditional instruction be moved outdoors. There are many concepts and objectives that are best learned in an indoor setting with the equipment and facilities that are readily available there. For example, in the descriptive writing example featured in The Natural Difference sidebar, the classroom was the appropriate place to define terms and present examples. An overuse of the outdoors can actually diminish the novelty of going to a different venue for learning.

Schoolyard-Enhanced Learning

The use of the outdoors surrounding the school to enhance instruction in a variety of content areas can be thought of as "schoolyard-enhanced learning." Although I hesitate to add another definition to the education lexicon, I feel that there needs to be a term that designates this specific aspect of the outdoor education concept. I see schoolyard-enhanced learning as an instructional strategy that uses the school site or adjacent areas to teach concepts and process skills from a variety of content areas. Following are some key elements of the term.

On-Site Location

Schoolyard-enhanced learning refers specifically to teaching activities that can take place right outside of the classroom. There is no need to arrange for a bus or wait for field trip permission forms to be returned. You are simply stepping outside.

Broad Range of Topics

Schoolyard-enhanced learning is not tied to a specific subject area. All content areas can benefit from an occasional change of pace and place. Sometimes the outdoors provides a great setting for learning—imagine sitting outside to write poetry on a warm afternoon. Or, the outdoors may serve as both venue and content—going out to estimate the heights of trees using indirect measurement techniques.

No Time Limit

Schoolyard-enhanced learning experiences can be of any length. Whether it's a quick trip outside to measure snow depth or a more lengthy, outdoor reflective writing experience, variety has been infused into the instructional routine, and learning has been enhanced.

Fresh Setting

Schoolyard-enhanced learning should be considered as one of many instructional approaches that can be used to add variety to teaching and learning. It is not meant to dominate instruction, but rather to provide a needed change of pace and place.

I have intentionally used the term *schoolyard* rather than *playground*. Although areas for both unstructured and structured play are very important, we need to focus on the entire school site as a possible instructional venue. The schoolyard needs to be viewed as more than just a play area; even the edges and unmowed grass can become sites for academic learning, reflection, community involvement, and recreation. My hope is that teachers will examine the curriculum and determine which learning objectives can be enhanced through the use of an outdoor setting.

Schoolyard-Enhanced Learning and Place-Based Education

In many ways, schoolyard-enhanced learning is a subset of place-based education. David Sobel, codirector of the Community-Based School Environmental Education Program, has defined place-based education as ". . . the process of using the local community and environment as a starting point to teach concepts in language arts, mathematics, social studies, science and other subjects across the curriculum" (2004, 7).

Place-based education is a comprehensive term that can include a variety of components such as internships, service learning, communitywide projects, environmental education, and so on.

Educational researcher Amy Powers says that place-based educators want ". . . to 'tear down' school walls so that the community becomes integral to all facets of student learning . . ." (2004, 18). Schoolyard-enhanced learning can certainly complement place-based education. If teachers feel comfortable going outside of the classroom to teach content concepts, there is a greater likelihood that they will venture beyond the schoolyard into the community for more in-depth projects. Correspondingly, when parents become accustomed to teaching that takes place outside of the school room, there is greater likelihood that they will accept a broadening of the instructional scope to the entire community.

Unfortunately, too often there is still the mind-set that real learning has to be classroom based. Schoolyard-enhanced learning can help to break down that notion and open the door (literally!) for more extensive community-based learning experiences. The Boston Schoolyard Initiative, for example, has been helping Boston schools for more than ten years to design and build schoolyards that provide a rich environment for teaching and learning. According to Chris Coxon, the Boston public schools deputy superintendent for teaching and learning, "Teachers learned that when you engage multiple senses of the child, the learning is deeper." (Boston Schoolyard Initiative 2005, 5)

The Benefits of Schoolyard-Enhanced Learning

Provide Concrete Experiences to Clarify Abstract Concepts

We were deep into the measurement unit. Although feet and yards were easy to visualize, the concept of an acre was troublesome. Oh, I dutifully wrote on the board that an acre equals 4,840 square yards, or 43,560 square feet, but the blank looks said it all. The next day, armed with reels of measuring tape borrowed from the athletic office, we went outside to measure an acre on the school grounds. First, we staked out an acre on the playground. Then we marked an acre on both the football field and the baseball diamond. The impact of these concrete examples was dramatic. Immediately, students began to estimate the acreage of the entire school grounds, as well as the approximate size of their own yards. A concrete outdoor experience had clarified an abstract concept.

In an era of standards and tests, we need to be able to justify the use of the outdoors from a pedagogical as well as an idealistic viewpoint. The use of the environment for teaching is well grounded in both theory and the experiences of practitioners.

Constructivism, as a description of how learning takes place, fits well with the concept of hands-on learning. One teacher describes learned knowledge and facts as having little hangers that need to be connected to something. The outdoors can be the "hook" that makes the connection solid. The process of actually measuring an acre outside provided a concrete connection for the concept of 4,840 square yards. After actually measuring an area the size of an acre, students were then able to build upon that understanding and relate it to other places based on their experience.

We teach a variety of abstract concepts that can often be powerfully augmented by the use of the outdoors. Concepts such as camouflage and protective coloration, for example, become much more meaningful when actually encountered in the natural world. And, as noted earlier, the concept of vivid description in language arts can be easily coaxed by focusing a writing activity outdoors on a sunny afternoon.

Provide Motivation for the Reluctant Learner

I have seen it myself—many times! A student who has a difficult time in the classroom suddenly becomes animated and involved with learning in an outdoor setting. Teachers who frequently use outdoor instruction have dozens of anecdotes that replay the same scenario. Perhaps the kids who blossom in an outdoor setting have a strong leaning toward Gardner's naturalist intelligence; or, perhaps these are kids who thrive on tactile/kinesthetic learning. Or, it may just be that some kids simply need a change of pace and place more than others.

Research is under way that may help to confirm years of teacher observations about how nature impacts our ability to work and think.

15

In an article in the *Journal of Environmental Psychology*, Stephen Kaplan summarizes some of his findings:

> *Directed attention plays an important role in human information processing; its fatigue, in turn, has far reaching consequences. Attention Restoration Theory provides an analysis of the kinds of experiences that lead to recovery from such fatigue. Natural environments turn out to be particularly rich in the characteristics necessary for restorative experiences. (1995, 169)*

Additional research is looking at more specific learning difficulties such as Attention Deficit Hyperactivity Disorder (ADHD). A variety of research projects are under way that may clarify more about the restorative role of nature and its impact on persons with learning difficulties. Important work in this area has been done by researchers at the Cornell University College of Human Ecology and the Human Environment Research Laboratory of the University of Illinois. A review of journals in both the special education and psychology literature shows the interest that exists in exploring the relationship of nature to learning.

Add Variety to Teaching and Learning

The phrase "a change of pace and a change of place" says it all. Implicit is the idea that students of any age need to experience a variety of instructional approaches. It's well established that the most effective teachers are comfortable using a variety of instructional approaches to teach the same concept. One researcher recommends that teachers present new content multiple times using a variety of input modes. Those modes can be either indirect experiences (such as reading or listening) or direct experiences (either real or a simulation) (Marzano 2003, 116).

The physical act of moving a class outdoors provides an immediate change of place and an opportunity for direct experience that can be motivating in and of itself. Being in a different environment can coax thinking down different avenues.

The outdoors does not have to be used just for teaching about things found there. I frequently will take a class outside simply to conduct a discussion. Of course, we could have done the same thing indoors, but there is something very energizing about moving to an outdoor setting, even if it is only a few feet from the school building. We all crave some variety and the outdoors can easily provide that change with a minimum of hassle.

Variety is important for the teacher as well as the student. I definitely feel a renewed enthusiasm when I occasionally change the venue for my teaching. Research studies also suggest that using the outdoors as an integrating context creates a renewed enthusiasm for teachers as well as students.

Although going outside provides an obvious change of place, it also can affect the pace of instruction. The richness of the outdoor environment naturally causes us to slow down a bit and react to our surroundings. It is certainly true that teaching a concept outdoors may take longer than "covering" the same content indoors, but much of that extra time comes from the closer inspection and reflection that is promoted by outdoor experiences.

The sights, sounds, smells, and textures of nature immediately pull at our senses. Especially for learners who are highly visual or tactile/kinesthetic, the outdoors can provide a rich variety of learning experiences. Unfortunately, because of passive indoor lifestyles, many students today do not have frequent opportunities to use their senses in the outdoors. By emphasizing outdoor activities that focus on observation skills, students can utilize their senses in a rich environment.

Help Increase Student Achievement

A key question must be asked in today's standards-based school environment: Does the use of the outdoors for instruction have an impact on student achievement? The question just can't be avoided. Are there positive learning outcomes that justify moving instruction beyond the classroom walls? It is extremely difficult to isolate outdoor instruction as a variable, especially when it is used as one of many instructional approaches in a teacher's repertoire.

Motivation and Enthusiasm Grow

A good beginning point is to ask how schoolyard-enhanced learning meshes with what we know as educational best practice. Robert Marzano's book *What Works in Schools: Translating Research*

17

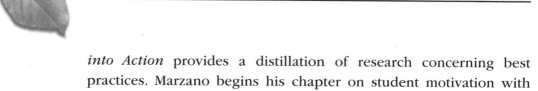

into Action provides a distillation of research concerning best practices. Marzano begins his chapter on student motivation with the following:

> *The link between student motivation and achievement is straightforward. If students are motivated to learn the content in a given subject, their achievement in that subject will most likely be good. (2003, 114)*

As he explores ways to enhance individual student motivation Marzano emphasizes that schools need to "provide students with tasks and activities that are inherently engaging" (2003, 149). The implication would be that if we can show that outdoor learning experiences are engaging and motivating, then there is certainly a greater likelihood that these experiences will contribute to student achievement gains. Two supporting examples come from opposite ends of the country.

A study of eleven Florida high schools specifically focused on the effects of environment-based education on students' achievement motivation. A comparison of achievement motivation was done with four hundred ninth- and twelfth-grade students, some of whom were in classrooms that used the environment as an integrating context (EIC) and others that were in traditional classrooms. After controlling for gender, grade point average, and ethnicity, the EIC groups had significantly higher achievement motivation (Place-Based Education Evaluation Collaborative, 2006).

The California Student Assessment Project examined eight paired classrooms of students, one of which utilized EIC approaches and the other did not. The EIC groups showed a greater enthusiasm for learning, and also demonstrated higher academic achievement than the non-EIC groups (State Education and Environment Roundtable 2006).

The Place-Based Education Evaluation Collaborative (PEEC) represents more than a dozen organizations that are conducting place-based programs primarily in New England–area schools. The PEEC website is an excellent source of general information regarding the effectiveness of place-based programming, and also provides information concerning student achievement research. The site gives brief summaries of research projects as well as links to the actual reports. I highly recommend the PEEC site for anyone looking for detailed documentation of research concerning the effectiveness of using the environment as an integrating context for instruction: http://www.peecworks.org.

One research study summarized on the PEEC site includes a report concerning four place-based education programs. The report includes survey results from 55 schools and 338 educators. The results are impressive:

> *Positive, statistically significant correlations were found between the amount of participant exposure to the program and nearly all desired outcomes, such as educator engagement/personal growth, ability to meet curricular goals , use of local resources for teaching, adult reports of student engagement learning and academic achievement, and student reports of attachment to place, time spent outdoors, and environmental stewardship behavior, among others. (2006)*

Gerald Lieberman and Linda Hoody were among the early researchers to focus on the environment as a learning context rather than as a curriculum topic. Their 1998 research study, published in a report titled *Closing the Achievement Gap: Using the Environment as an Integrating Context for Learning*, found intriguing data that definitely support the use of the outdoors for instruction. Their study included forty schools from thirteen states, representing all grade levels (K–12). The outcomes indicate that students learn more within an environment-based context than within a traditional educational framework.

It is important to emphasize that Lieberman and Hoody were not just focusing on environmental education. Their research focused on the concept of "using the environment as an integrating context" (frequently referred to as EIC), which meant that teachers were using "a school's surroundings and community as a framework within which students [could] construct their own learning, guided by teachers and administrators using proven educational practices" (1998, 7).

The study showed encouraging benefits associated with instruction that moved beyond the classroom walls:

- better performance on standardized measures of academic achievement in reading, writing, math, science, and social studies
- reduced discipline and classroom management problems
- increased engagement and enthusiasm for learning
- greater pride and ownership in accomplishments

(1998)

The results mentioned in *Closing the Achievement Gap* certainly make sense to anyone who has used the outdoors as a teaching tool. For example, in language arts, the study reported greater enthusiasm for the subject, improved development of language arts skills, and increased success in communicating with others (Lieberman and Hoody 1998). It truly makes sense—as students become involved with experiences that interest them, there is a greater interest in communicating through both the spoken and written word.

Language arts concepts seem more immediate and compelling when you are trying to share what you have experienced in the environment. I know of a high school where students enthusiastically began a letter-writing campaign (yes, *letters*, not emails!) when a cell phone tower was proposed for a community park. Most teens wouldn't jump at the chance to write a letter, but when the problem affected their "place," both the mechanics and power of writing took on new meaning.

Improved Understanding

In mathematics, research found that students had "an improved understanding of mathematical concepts and content," "better mastery of math skills," and were "more enthusiastic for studying math" (Lieberman and Hoody 1998). The key elements again are relevance, application, and enthusiasm. As mathematical concepts are applied in real-world settings, students can make the connection between abstract concepts and practical application. The math becomes a tool to use, rather than an exercise to complete.

Every spring, one Ohio middle grades teacher has students figure out how much fertilizer the custodian will need to apply to the school lawn. This rather complex project involves first determining the total area of the school site and then subtracting spaces such as parking lots, ball fields, and wood chip–covered play areas. Instead of a tedious textbook exercise in measurement and area, the topic is transformed into a class project that clarifies math concepts, hones math skills, and creates a general enthusiasm for a math assignment.

Although achievement gains and the fostering of higher-order thinking skills are the frequently mentioned findings in the Lieberman and Hoody study, another outcome is sometimes overlooked. It is very significant that teachers who used the outdoors as an integrating context also experienced revitalized attitudes toward teaching. Teachers, like students, need variety. The use of the outdoors for teaching can provide the change that can energize a teacher and consequently the student. I can't help but wonder how many of those achievement gains were fueled in part because the teacher had a renewed vitality for teaching. An elementary teacher recently said to me, "I'm so enthusiastic when I'm outdoors; and when I'm enthusiastic, the kids are, too!"

Research studies that isolate achievement gains resulting from the use of the schoolyard as a teaching resource are difficult to find. However, the positive research findings concerning environment-based education and place-based education should have some relevance to schoolyard-enhanced learning. All three concepts involve moving students beyond the four walls of the classroom. All three learning strategies also emphasize relevance and student engagement. As Marzano notes, engagement is essential to foster student motivation, which, in turn, is related to achievement (2003).

Much of the research that has been done in the recent past has been quite global in perspective, attempting to analyze a number of variables in an environment-based learning context. The results of those studies have been very positive and certainly indicate that both teaching and learning can benefit from the greater use of the world beyond the school walls. In the future, as one report notes, there is a need ". . . to systematically explore the ways that *specific* teaching practices lead to *specific* types of student achievement" (Duffin et al. 2004, 26).

Compatible with Many Current Practices in Education

Inquiry Teaching

Michael Rest, a middle grades science teacher in Baltimore, writes this beautiful description of the inquiry process:

This is where science begins. Students must be able to recognize what exists and happens in the world around them, first identifying what is normally in place, or growing, or occurring in their world, then making note of what is changing. Once patterns emerge, they become surprised with the unexpected. Questions arise. Investigations ensue. (Bourne 2000, 95)

Although he is specifically referring to science, the process of inquiring knows no content-area boundaries. What Rest is identifying are two critical process skills:

1) observation: recognizing what is existing and happening; identifying what is normally happening and what appears to be changing

2) analysis: identifying emerging patterns

The schoolyard environment is an ideal setting in which to reinforce these critical concepts. Whether students are engaged in a science experiment, literary analysis, mathematical operations, or historical research, they need to have strong observation and analysis skills.

Inquiry teaching is characterized by questioning. Both students and teacher pose questions. Emphasis is placed on gathering evidence to support explanations and learners are encouraged to communicate and justify their explanations. Of course, inquiry teaching can be effectively done indoors; but once again, focusing an inquiry activity outside adds that important change of pace and place.

Susan Cook took her students outside to look at several examples of erosion that were taking place on the school grounds. Immediately, "erosion" was no longer a vocabulary word to be memorized but was linked to a real problem at the school. Both students and teachers posed questions, and students gathered evidence of the problem and then began to formulate explanations of what had caused the erosion problems at the school. Students then went to the next level and worked on possible solutions for the problem, including the designations of different routes for students to use when leaving the building.

Block and Flexible Scheduling

Schoolyard-enhanced learning works very well with schedules that can be modified to permit more than the standard fifty-minute class period. A ninety-minute block of time is ample to provide for both indoor and outdoor activities in the same class session.

A block-scheduled class that relies on a constant dose of lecture/ discussion is doomed. The effective use of block scheduling requires that the teacher vary the instructional approaches. Occasional outdoor teaching can provide the necessary change of pace and place to keep motivation high. And, as we saw before, high motivation is associated with increased student achievement.

Higher-Order Thinking Skills

Identifying Similarities and Differences

Going outside doesn't "teach" higher-order thinking skills. Rather, it provides a venue of rich experiences from which the elements of Bloom's cognitive domain can be coaxed. For example, the concept of protective coloration, first learned indoors as a definition at the knowledge level, can be comprehended outside by having students find different colors of pipe cleaners randomly distributed on the schoolyard. Students can then apply their knowledge of camouflage as they look for examples of protective coloration in nature. They then can analyze the results of the pipe cleaner activity in terms of the types of protective coloration that they found outside.

Responding and Valuing

Schoolyard-enhanced learning is also very compatible with the affective domain. Responding, valuing, organizing, and characterizing are processes that can be easily utilized in outdoor teaching. Indeed, it may well be that the affective domain is the best suited to outdoor learning activities. A child who has had extensive exposure to the outdoors will hopefully grow to value the natural world and characterize his or her behavior with a stewardship ethic. You won't be concerned about habitat destruction if you have never explored your own backyard.

Multiple Intelligences

Howard Gardner's work (1993) concerning multiple intelligences (MI) has had a tremendous impact upon instructional planning over the last two decades. The concept that "intelligence" can be identified in ways other than just verbal or mathematical aptitude has generated both controversy as well as acceptance.

Gardner's addition of a naturalist intelligence in 1996 was very affirming, but really only confirmed what outdoor educators had

23

been seeing for many years. The naturalist intelligence refers to the ability to carefully observe in the natural environment and be able to discriminate even subtle differences. Someone with a strong naturalist intelligence is able to observe patterns in the natural world and can categorize the natural phenomena that have been observed.

Bruce Campbell, a teacher and MI consultant, mentions a number of instructional strategies that play to the naturalist intelligence. Activities such as collecting data and objects from the natural world, observing nature, using magnifiers or microscopes to study nature, keeping notebooks, and noticing changes in nature all are compatible with the naturalist intelligence. Of course, the naturalist intelligence can be emphasized via indoor activities also, but the outdoors is especially suited for activities centering around this intelligence (2005).

Looking Ahead

My purpose for writing this book can be very simply stated: to encourage you to use the most powerful audio-visual tool around—the outdoors. Although the book focuses on teachers and schools, it is intended to be useful to anyone with an interest in working with children in the outdoors: nature center staff, camp program directors, homeschooling parents, leaders of youth organizations, and so on.

In the chapters that follow, the emphasis is on practical examples, suggestions, and activities that can facilitate schoolyard-enhanced learning. A variety of exemplary classroom teachers have contributed their activities and suggestions for moving beyond the classroom walls. *Schoolyard-Enhanced Learning* provides both a rationale for outdoor instruction as well as the practical nuts and bolts that are needed to make it work. Following is a quick overview of the book.

Chapter 1 sets the stage for outdoor teaching and assists you in convincing others about the value of the concept. The chapter provides a brief overview of the educational theory and societal context that surrounds and supports outdoor instruction. It also explores the benefits of schoolyard-enhanced learning and reviews examples of research related to place-based learning.

Chapter 2 focuses on a very practical question: How do I make the schoolyard an inviting and functional outdoor classroom? The chapter shares very specific ideas for developing the schoolyard into a useful learning space. It explores topics such as planning, site enhancement, attracting wildlife, school gardens, maintenance, funding, and community resources.

Chapter 3 tackles the specifics of how to work with your class in the outdoors. After an introductory section that discusses ways to build and maintain administrative and parent support for outdoor learning, the chapter is organized around three major themes: things to consider before going outside; ways to make the most of your time while outdoors; and ways to build upon the outdoor experience back in the classroom.

Chapters 4 and 5 present a variety of teacher-tested activities that utilize schoolyard-enhanced learning. Chapter 4 focuses on ways to teach process skills that are common to many areas of study. Chapter 5 provides examples of outdoor activities that are related to specific subject areas.

Chapter 6 offers a variety of suggestions for making the most of the outdoors. The topics, including "Making the Most of a Hike," "The GPS as a Teaching Tool," "Resident Outdoor Education," and "Initiative Tasks," provide a wealth of options for teachers who are interested in taking schoolyard-enhanced learning to the next level.

An Opportunity

Although we are living in an era of media and activity saturation, schools can provide some alternative opportunities. For many kids, nature is a novelty. When hands-on outdoor experiences are woven into instruction, students are quickly engaged and motivated to examine the world around them. The simple act of moving a language arts lesson to the lawn on a warm September afternoon can provide an opportunity for relaxed reflection that may not be frequently modeled even at home.

Using the outdoors for learning is not a new idea. Artwork from ancient Greece shows teachers and pupils learning in small groups outside. As the centuries passed, however, "school" became identified with an indoor setting. Bigger groups of students were easier to manage in a confined space and learning became more associated with memorization than with experience. We still have remnants today of the concept that "real" learning should not be pleasant.

But "real" learning with a positive spin is taking place right outside the classroom door in schools across the country and, indeed, around the world. Abstract concepts are being clarified, reluctant learners motivated, and variety is being infused into instruction. The result— increases in achievement and greater student enthusiasm. Now that truly is "real" learning!

Chapter 2

Making the School Grounds an Outdoor Classroom

"Imagine a classroom with sky for a ceiling and earth for a floor. A room without walls or desks, where young scientists explore the world of bugs; mathematicians measure rainfall; budding writers record their observations; and actors rehearse on a natural stage."

—Boston Schoolyard Initiative

Creating a classroom that has the "sky for a ceiling and earth for a floor" is really not as unrealistic as it first sounds. Schoolyard-enhanced learning does not require a large tract of land or sophisticated landscaping. In fact, one school in downtown Boston, completely surrounded by concrete, actually created an outdoor learning environment with a variety of container gardens on the rooftop! A teacher in urban Cleveland has students inventory and monitor the changes in plants growing through the network of meandering cracks on the asphalt playground.

The schoolyard should be an adventure waiting to happen. Unfortunately, schoolyards are frequently associated with parking spaces, ball fields, and the standard-issue plastic and metal play equipment. When green space does exist, it is regularly groomed and trimmed like a traditional lawn.

Why Create a Special Outdoor Learning Space?

A dozen multicolored snakes peeked from the foliage in the school garden plot. Students made the snakes from paper, colored them, and then hid the paper critters to blend in with the immediate surroundings as shown in Figure 2.1. The challenge was to try and find all of the "snakes" in the garden.

Figure 2.1 Camouflage becomes more than an abstract concept when students decorate paper "snakes" to blend in with their surroundings. Can you spot the critter hidden in the blooms?

The activity was an extension of an indoor discussion about camouflage in nature. Could the concept have been taught indoors? Sure. Did the outdoor component make the concept more real? Absolutely! You can be sure that when these kids hear the word *camouflage*, they will think back to the colorful snakes they created and hid in the garden.

The major advantage of an outdoor learning space is that it enhances the options open to a teacher. For me, the key word is variety. When a mix of teaching methods is used, there is a greater probability that more students will be motivated to learn. The research cited in Chapter 1 emphasizes that motivated students achieve well. If kids are engaged, they will be motivated, and there is no doubt in my mind that the outdoors is a highly engaging place.

That's the beauty of outdoor teaching. The outdoors can serve as the venue for learning, or as the content. You win either way! Taking a class outside for forty-five minutes can provide the variety needed to engage kids in the content being taught.

Transforming the Schoolyard

This chapter includes many specific ideas and resources for transforming the schoolyard into an exciting and functional learning environment. Of course, every situation is different. Some schools are blessed with large open spaces bordered by trees and fields, while others feel fortunate to have even a small patch of grass. Older, urban schools often face unique challenges such as very limited green space and neglected school grounds that are often vandalized.

28

The Boston Schoolyard Initiative (BSI) is a magnificent example of how one major urban center utilized public-private partnerships to realize a mission of transforming schoolyards into "dynamic centers for learning and community life" (2001, 1). In its first ten years of operation, BSI constructed sixty-one new schoolyards for schools of all grade levels located throughout Boston's diverse neighborhoods.

The BSI has conceptualized the word *schoolyard* in a way that embraces both a definition and a philosophy:

> *A schoolyard is a school's "external environment," whether large or small, beautiful or unsightly, actively used or completely abandoned. Whatever its condition, a schoolyard is an indicator of the health of the surrounding community, and each has a powerful impact on the other. An unimproved or degraded schoolyard sends a negative message about the school and the neighborhood in which it is situated. A dynamic and active schoolyard adds to the vibrancy of both. (2001, 11)*

Although the BSI definition of a schoolyard could apply in any setting, it has special meaning in urban environments where schools and their neighborhoods blend almost as one. For more information about the BSI, check their website at: http://www.schoolyards.org.

Whether you are planning to create an extensive land laboratory or are just looking for a few simple features to include on the school grounds, this chapter is meant to prime the pump by providing a framework for planning. The goal is to show examples of things that teachers have tried as schoolyard enhancements; there is no ideal configuration for every school. Only you and your administration can decide what is appropriate, useful, and safe for your specific location, students, staff, neighborhood, climate, and topography.

Schoolyard-enhanced learning is so practical and convenient because it requires only stepping outside the door. It isn't necessary to have a meticulously designed land laboratory with sophisticated learning stations. By adding just a few simple features, the schoolyard can become a viable outdoor teaching space.

Both simple and complex schoolyard enhancement projects benefit when some basic concepts are included in the planning process. If the schoolyard is to be welcoming, useful, and naturally intriguing it needs to incorporate several elements:

- functional instructional spaces
- variety of plants, animals, and natural features
- aesthetically pleasing elements
- maintenance and logistical considerations

Functional Instructional Spaces

The two most important words related to school site enhancement are *flexibility* and *variety*. If the schoolyard is to be used easily and frequently for both planned and impromptu experiences, it has to be a functional, interesting, and comfortable place. To maximize the impact of outdoor teaching, it makes sense to avoid making the outdoor classroom configuration too similar to the indoor setting. I have seen some outdoor teaching/meeting areas that are just rows of fixed benches and tables with a teacher table in front—way too similar to the indoor environment! As you plan outdoor teaching stations, try to take full advantage of the outdoor setting and the flexibility it provides.

It's very useful to designate an area outside where students can sit and also have surfaces on which to lay out materials or write. These spaces can be as simple or elaborate as budget and time permit. The area serves as a hub or home base for explaining activities, distributing materials, and sharing findings. Many teachers find that having a specific outdoor teaching/meeting area provides a structure to the outdoor experience and focuses student attention. Following are some points to ponder when planning a teaching/meeting area.

The Space

How Frequently Will the Space Be Used?

In most cases, a teaching/meeting area that is close to the building increases the likelihood of usage. It's important, though, to keep the teaching/meeting area away from heavily used play locations and equipment that could be distracting. If the school site has interesting natural features that will be frequently utilized, like woods or a wetland area, it is helpful to also have a work area near these features.

What Size Should It Be?

Consider what the average size group will be that will utilize the area. For most purposes, a teaching/meeting area that can accommodate the usual class size in your building should be adequate. Some schools have created simple mini-amphitheaters to provide a venue for large group presentations or work. A gentle slope can be converted into seating space that provides an outdoor performance venue.

30

Will Seating Configuration Need to Change?

How important is it to be able to change the seating configuration? This question needs to be considered carefully since it has a direct impact on flexibility. Commercially installed fixed seating looks very attractive, but can also greatly limit how the space will be used. As a general rule, opt for the most flexibility possible. Benches that can be easily moved, or even log seating, make it possible to configure a variety of work groups in your teaching/meeting space.

How Important Are Flat Work Surfaces?

Although clipboards and lapboards can serve as portable tables, it also is very helpful to have work surfaces where students can lay out materials, write, or just keep items off the ground. Students often bring materials back to the meeting area, or work on activities that are best done on a hard surface. If at all possible, try to incorporate both seating and work surface into a teaching/meeting area.

How Much Money Can We Spend?

This question should probably be answered first! The good news is that the teaching/meeting area does not need to be expensive. For example, natural materials such as logs and boulders are both aesthetically pleasing and cheap! Consider, also, partnering with an industrial arts teacher or vocational school and explore the possibility of having some seating or tables produced by high school students.

Where Should the Teaching/Meeting Area Be Placed?

The answer, of course, is highly dependent on the configuration of your site. Try to anticipate what natural areas will be the most heavily used—lawn, field, garden plots, wooded areas, wetland, and so on. As much as possible, the teaching/meeting area should be placed in a location that is somewhat central to the most used areas. If there is an important natural feature such as a woodlot that is not right next to the school, consider setting up a second staging area.

In many cases, the lawn will be the most frequently used locale. You may want to locate the teaching/meeting area near a door. An instructional area that is close to an entrance saves time as students move outside and also avoids a "recess mentality" that can occur if students have to walk a distance to the outdoor teaching area. Another

31

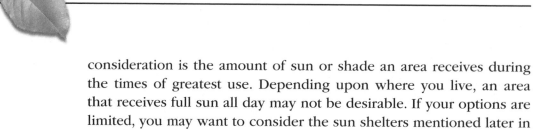

consideration is the amount of sun or shade an area receives during the times of greatest use. Depending upon where you live, an area that receives full sun all day may not be desirable. If your options are limited, you may want to consider the sun shelters mentioned later in the chapter.

Seating

To maximize the use of time outdoors and to make the outdoors practical as an instructional site, it is important to have some type of seating area that can accommodate a class of students. Figures 2.2a, b, and c show some examples. Following is a listing of some possible options.

Benches

Advantages: Benches come in a wide variety of styles and sizes, with many produced from recycled materials. If the benches are relatively lightweight, they can be readily moved to accommodate various groupings and can be easily stacked and stored. If you are planning to purchase benches, compare the cost of benches both with and without backs. If the difference isn't too much for the budget, you may want to purchase at least a few comfortable benches with backs.

Disadvantages: There are very few disadvantages to lightweight benches. Although there is no writing surface, small benches can easily be pulled up to any table or work area. The only downside is cost. Although purchased benches can be expensive, there is a tremendous range of styles, materials, and prices. As was mentioned earlier, high school industrial arts classes or vocational schools may be willing to help you with your project.

Picnic Tables

Advantages: Picnic tables can serve as both seating and work space. Some convertible table designs allow them to be used as either a table with an attached bench, or a bench with a full back.

Picnic tables come in a wide variety of sizes and styles and make great projects for parents who want to help but have limited carpentry skills. Since picnic tables also give a parklike look to a setting, they are an excellent choice for an outdoor area that encourages community use.

Disadvantages: Picnic tables usually occupy considerable space and are heavy to move around on a site. If you plan to change the seating configuration frequently, or plan to stack and store the tables during low-use times of the year, heavy tables and benches may not be practical.

Logs—Upright or Horizontal

Advantages: Logs are a great seating option. You can use small sections (1 foot to 3 feet high) placed vertically, or long sections of logs placed horizontally on the ground or mounted a short distance off the ground. Varied log heights efficiently accommodate varied student heights. The logs can be easily moved into any configuration and blend beautifully with an outdoor setting. The price is right, too—if you put out the word, you will probably be overwhelmed with parents, pickup trucks, and free wood. If you are using upright sections, be sure that the logs are wide enough to provide comfortable seating and stability.

Disadvantages: The biggest disadvantage is comfort. The absence of a backrest can make sitting for long periods of time a bit uncomfortable. But if we're going outdoors, we shouldn't be sitting in seats for a long time—right?

Flat Rocks or Boulders

Advantages: Boulders blend perfectly with a natural setting. If you can obtain a variety of types, you have an instant collection of specimens to use when teaching geology! Kids also really enjoy climbing on rocks. With many grooves and textures, rocks make a fantastic perch for the tactile kinesthetic child.

33

Figures 2.2a, 2.2b, and 2.2c Outdoor seating is a practical addition to the schoolyard and helps to create a defined instructional space. Logs and boulders are very inexpensive options if benches or tables are not in the budget.

Disadvantages: There are several disadvantages, with discomfort heading the list. Boulders are just not comfortable and create a more cumbersome seat than do logs. Safety also has to be a consideration.

Aside from the comfort factor, another disadvantage is the difficulty in obtaining and relocating suitably sized boulders. Boulders of adequate size to serve as seats have to be big, and usually require special equipment to transport and position them on the site. Also, once the boulders are in place, they will stay there—it's extremely difficult to reconfigure a seating arrangement once the rocks are in place.

Work Surfaces

To make an outdoor site practical, flexible, and easy to use, it is important to have a work surface in the teaching/meeting area. At the very minimum, there should be some type of raised flat surface that can be used by the teacher as a table to keep materials or equipment off the ground.

Whether or not to include student table space primarily revolves around cost and site considerations. Commercially produced all-weather tables to accommodate a classroom can be expensive. Finding adequate space for a grouping of tables outdoors also can be difficult on a small site. Many schools have used picnic tables to provide both seating and a student work surface. Flat benches can be used for writing or sorting and also double as seating. If tables or benches do not fit into your budget, clipboards can always provide a low-cost option for a student work surface.

An Inexpensive Seating Option: Sit-Upons

These are cushions or pads made of waterproof material. You place them on the ground and "sit upon" them. (Girl Scouts came up with this one decades ago!) One simple way to make a sit-upon is to take a gallon-size freezer storage bag, insert several layers of newspaper or packing foam "peanuts," remove as much air as possible, and seal. For backsides that might exceed the dimensions of a gallon freezer bag, sturdy plastic bags holding layers of newspaper and sealed with duct tape work well and can be made to varying sizes.

An Internet search on *sit-upon* yields dozens of ideas for making these handy outdoor seats. But easiest of all—if you don't want to stuff or sew, stadium cushions also work very well.

Sit-upons are inexpensive and very portable. You can have kids sit anywhere and always stay dry. If kids take along clipboards, you have both dry seating and a writing surface always ready for use in any location.

Sun Shelters

If natural shade is not available to shield your outdoor study area, you may want to consider constructing a sun shelter. Peterborough, Ontario, teacher Drew Monkman describes an A-frame, post-and-beam structure that measures approximately 21 feet by 21 feet, with a sloping roof that ranges from 7 to 10 feet high. The structure is just a roof supported by four columns—there are no walls. The shelter looks like an open picnic pavilion and contains bench seating for up to fifty students. The floor is just the lawn.

A sun shelter can enhance a study site in several ways. Although sunshine is great, it is possible to have too much of a good thing—especially on a hot afternoon in May or late August. The sun shelter provides a retreat while still maintaining connection with the outdoors. A shelter can also encourage greater use of the outdoors for teaching. As Monkman notes, "The structure creates a defined teaching space where students can concentrate with less distraction, and some teachers report a greater sense of class control—an important point since fear of lack of control is one reason why many teachers hesitate to take their students outside" (Monkman 2001).

Interpretive Signage

If your site has unique features, consider putting up unobtrusive signs or identification labels. An unusual tree, animal home, geologic feature, or observation area will be more easily incorporated into teaching if it is identified. Signs also can point out a walking route as well as indicate areas that are off limits. As you consider signage, remember that a site cluttered with labels quickly loses its feeling of "wild and natural." Label only unique features that could be easily missed.

An option that is less expensive and more vandal resistant than text and picture signage is to use unobtrusive posts with numbers routed into them to indicate points of interest. The numbers are then keyed to a paper guide that teachers have in their classrooms.

Variety of Plants, Animals, and Natural Features

Although functional instructional work areas are important, the heart of outdoor teaching is found in the natural elements that are incorporated into the site. Although it is possible to walk out of most any school building and do some outdoor teaching, there are many simple enhancements that can make the school grounds an even richer source of experiences and venues.

To create a useful and engaging outdoor learning site, it's essential to provide as much variety as possible. Outdoor learning activities can take place on a manicured lawn, but the diversity found in such a monoculture is limited. The more plants, animals, and natural features that are available, the easier it is to develop a variety of instructional opportunities. A useful way to think of the outdoor classroom is to view the schoolyard as a habitat.

The National Wildlife Federation (NWF) has focused on backyard and schoolyard habitat development for more than thirty years. The NWF Schoolyard Habitats program can provide an excellent framework from which to enhance a school site. As teachers plan enhancements to the school site, the NWF encourages thinking in terms of the four elements that are essential to wildlife:

food

cover

places to raise young

water

These four elements are excellent organizers for planning schoolyard enhancements.

Food

Vegetation can provide for the food needs of many animals. The plants on your site also have a tremendous impact on the types of learning activities that you can utilize. Choosing plants that are native to your area provides many advantages. According to the NWF, choosing native plants will:

- *provide the best overall food sources for wildlife*
- *require less water and overall maintenance*
- *support ten to fifty times as many species of native wildlife as nonnative plants*
- *help maintain the diversity of plant species in our communities*
- *educate students about high-quality restoration work*
  (2007)

The NWF even includes an interactive web page that allows you to click on your state and see the top ten plants for your region of the country: http://www.nwf.org/backyard/food.cfm.

The task of discovering what plants are native to your state is a worthwhile learning activity that integrates well into local history units. An Internet search using the term: "(your state) native plants" will yield an abundance of lists, often including pictures of local plants. The Lady Bird Johnson Wildflower Center (www.wildflower.org) is a wonderfully comprehensive site that provides links to just about everything you might want to know about native plants.

As always, the key word is variety. For maximum diversity, as well as maximum interest and teaching flexibility, try to utilize many different plant materials. Robin Moore, in his book *Plants for Play,* has some excellent guidelines for providing variety in an outdoor environment:

- *Vary the texture of leaves: evergreen with deciduous; shiny with rough; serrated with smooth edges; thin with thick.*
- *Vary the form, size and shape of plants.*
- *Select plants that emphasize seasonal change: evergreen contrasted with deciduous; seasonal color; early leaves; late flowers; seeds, nuts and fruits.*
- *Consider opportunities for color in trees, ground covers, vines, annuals and perennials.*
- *Select plants for fragrance.*
- *Select plants for craft and culinary activities.*
- *Select plants for auditory stimulation. Some plants, especially in the fall, produce interesting sounds when the wind blows through their dry leaves. (1993, 4–5)*

37

Cover and Places to Raise Young

Plantings often can provide both food and cover for birds and other animals. It's important to have a wide variety of plantings to provide protection both from predators and the elements. Think of cover in terms of layers. On the ground, rotting logs and decaying plant material can provide valuable cover to a multitude of small critters. Plants of varying heights fill the needs of yet other animals. Tall trees can provide a canopy that provides cover of another sort. Once again, variety is the key.

When a mowed area meets an unmowed area, an edge effect is created. Similar to the concept of an ecotone, this transitional area can contain some species from both mini habitats. Edge effects can be excellent learning sites. The mowed area makes the site very accessible and students can quickly see the differences and similarities that are found in both.

The Ohio Department of Natural Resources (ODNR) Division of Wildlife's Wild School Site Project has some wonderful ideas for coaxing wildlife to the school grounds. Not only are these projects relatively easy to do, but they can be done for practically no cost. Following are a few excerpts from their award-winning book, *Twenty/Twenty: Projects and Activities for Wild School Sites* (1996), written and compiled by Paul Schiff and reprinted here with permission.

"Beautiful Brush Piles"

Fallen or pruned tree limbs can provide cover for small mammals. Branches can be arranged in a crisscrossed pattern with the largest boughs on the bottom, forming a mound 3 to 5 feet high. Some drainage tile placed at the base of the pile can make the pile safer for small mammals. Maximum use of the brush pile occurs when it is placed near a feeding station (but not too close—you want predators to have to work a little harder for their food!). Although brush piles appear a bit unsightly, a small interpretive sign explaining the function can help to legitimize their presence.

"There's Life in Dead Trees"

A rotting log is a must for a schoolyard habitat! If none are available on the site, consider locating one and find someone with a pickup truck to bring it to your site. It's ideal if you can place the log in a shaded, moist location. Actually, several logs in varying stages of decay make for great cover, and can provide wonderful contrasts.

"Mower Less"

An open area that is left unmowed can provide excellent habitat for rabbits, some species of birds, and small mammals such as the meadow vole. Although the unmowed area on your school site will probably not be large enough to attract large numbers of meadow dwellers, it can serve as a useful demonstration plot. Look for an area that receives full sun and is easy to access. Leave the plot unmowed through winter to provide food and shelter for wildlife. Some folks like to mow the plot in early spring, prior to the emergence of new growth. If your plot is large enough, consider mowing a strip down the middle for greater access.

Placement of the unmowed area is usually the biggest hurdle. Since our culture places a high premium on neatly mowed lawns, your unmowed demonstration plot can stick out like the proverbial sore thumb. It's crucial to talk with maintenance staff and administrators to determine what area would cause the least problems in terms of

Wildlife

Habitat Restoration

Area and

Study Site

Figure 2.3 It's amazing how a simple sign can help the public to perceive an overgrown area as a study site rather than a weed patch.

both mowing and public relations. An official-looking sign such as the one shown in Figure 2.3 delineates the area as a study site, which will silence critics and create interest!

You may have to start small and be creative. I know of one teacher who first staked off a small area to keep unmowed. Then, every few weeks, he quietly moved the stakes out another 6 inches!

"Rocks and Boulders"

Adding a rock pile to your school site can yield many worthwhile results. A variety of animals such as ground-feeding birds, amphibians, reptiles, and chipmunks utilize rocky areas both as a source of cover and a place to raise young. Passageways and entrance tunnels can be simulated with scrap pipe or tile.

Rocks also are good teaching materials. Colonization by lichens and other plants provides students an opportunity to see the first stages of soil building. How large should the rocks be? "Too large to pick up and throw, yet small enough to be handled."

"Animal Tracking Plot"

Animal tracks always attract attention. A tracking plot can be made by simply clearing an area—at least 3 feet by 3 feet—of all grass and vegetation. Then, cover the area with clay soil. You may have to experiment with locally available clay, clay/soil or clay/sand to see which holds an impression best. It takes about three gallons of clay per square foot. The tracking plot will look neater if it is framed with lumber that is buried level with the surface of the ground. The area in the frame is then dug out and filled with clay. You can experiment with different types of "bait" to see what critters are visiting your site. The tracks can even be preserved using photographs or plaster of Paris poured into a paper collar placed around the track.

Water

This major habitat component may not be in abundance on your school site. If you are fortunate enough to have a small pond, stream, or wetland on or adjacent to your schoolyard, consider yourself blessed!

Most animals will not limit their range to your schoolyard, so it is not essential that you provide an open water source. On the other hand, the provision of some clean, fresh water can increase the number of visitors to your site.

The simplest way to provide water is with some form of the traditional birdbath. Placing some small stones in the basin will also make it more attractive to small birds who avoid deeper water. Providing water at different heights attracts different types of animals. Place a few water receptacles directly on the ground—any shallow pan or tray placed on the ground near shrubbery or cover is effective. If you do decide to provide watering locations on your site, it's critical that the water stay clean and fresh. You're asking for trouble, both for wildlife and your program, if you have a bunch of containers of stagnant water sitting around the school grounds!

To provide water in a grander fashion, consider small plastic pond liners available in garden stores, or even the construction of a shallow pond on the site. However, the addition of a water feature of even very shallow depth always opens the door for questions concerning safety and liability. It is essential that any plans for a water feature going beyond birdbath proportions be thoroughly discussed with school officials.

Aesthetically Pleasing Elements

We want to attract animals to the school site, but it's also important to attract people. While there is no need to create a perfectly sculpted garden spot, some attention to basic aesthetics is prudent. Parents and community members frequently form strong impressions of a school from only cursory glimpses of the building and grounds.

More than once, I've heard a parent say, "We have a good school— look how well kept it is." Of course, outward appearances (of both people and schools!) can be deceiving, but the fact remains that the image conveyed by the school grounds is important. Although we know that brush piles are great habitats for little critters, aesthetically it might be best to place the pile behind the building. And that composting area might work just as well at the corner of the property rather than at the edge of the visitor parking area.

Following are a few other suggestions for making the schoolyard inviting and visitor friendly.

Pathways

Well-planned pathways lead people to interesting elements on the school site such as feeding stations, rotting logs, or unmowed study plots. In its most basic form, a pathway might simply be a mowed area that threads through tall grass. Pathways can also be made with a variety of materials such as wood chips, asphalt, or crushed limestone. Crushed limestone combined with dust-like limestone screenings hardens to a very durable surface that is naturally slip resistant.

A school in Boston uses stepping "stones," which are actually slices of a tree trunk or large limb. Not only do the tree cookies provide a place to step, they also can serve as a visual for talking about the age of trees. The stepping-stone approach is much less expensive than paving or using limestone, although the inserts need to be securely set in the soil to avoid creating wobbly surfaces and a tripping hazard.

Pathways help to keep foot traffic confined to specific areas and prevent erosion and the trampling of plant material. Consider using a variety of possible path layouts. A mix of straight-line paths and meandering walkways creates visual interest and can actually make a small site seem bigger. You need to also consider if you wish to add a border or edging to the paths. Accessibility for students with disabilities always needs to be a primary concern and should be a key factor in determining path width and surface.

Pathway Benches

If your site is large enough, you may want to consider adding a few benches along the pathways. Benches come in a variety of materials and styles, including many recycled models.

Because benches should be sturdy and need to be fastened securely to the ground, they can be rather expensive. One Ohio school has devised an innovative way to provide seating without incurring a large cost. The Wooster High School site incorporates benches that have been given in honor or memory of an individual or group. A small metal plate acknowledges the honoree and the donor. It's a great way to commemorate or celebrate persons or groups that are part of the school and community. The same concept can be used for obtaining trees. The donated tree can be acknowledged with a small plaque, or as one school does, a book of tree donations is kept in a permanent location and lists both honoree and donor, as well as information about the tree species. This can be a very effective and inexpensive way to develop a grove of trees on the property.

Identification

Figure 2.4 Visitors can check the bulletin board for information about the site, as well as regulations concerning usage.

A sign that names or designates the outdoor learning area can be a good way to inform the community that you are using the outdoors for instruction. The signage may be as simple as a wooden plaque that just names the area, or it may be more complex and also include a diagram showing the layout of the outdoor instructional features on the site. Whether the sign is simple or detailed, it should have a professional look and be both weather and vandal resistant. As shown in Figure 2.4, some schools have used a small outdoor bulletin board to both identify the site and also provide seasonal interpretive information about the plants and animals that are on the site, as well as information about ongoing work or studies that are taking place.

A simple sign often can say a lot. Kidron Elementary School conducted a "name the land lab" contest as their new garden and study area was under construction. Students eagerly contributed entries which added momentum to the already exciting project. The winning name—Nature's Nest—says it all!

Artwork in the Schoolyard

Figure 2.5 A school in Boston had students help to create mosaics that were beautifully incorporated into a walkway.

The outdoors can be a great place to include artistic elements. Student work such as murals, painted graphics, and sculptures can be beautifully incorporated into an outdoor setting, as can be seen in Figure 2.5. Building walls and seating areas can provide the background for artwork. Benches also can be utilized as canvas for the outdoor artist. If you are uneasy about applying paint to the building wall, use panels that can be attached and changed from time to time.

The schoolyard is also a great place to incorporate environmental sculpture, which uses natural materials and surroundings to create an art form. This form of art, often associated with artist and photographer Andy Goldsworthy, can provide a meaningful addition to the school site.

Gates and Fences

The decision whether to have fences around the schoolyard was probably made long before you decided to develop an outdoor learning site. Urban schools usually are more likely to have fencing surrounding the grounds. Fencing can be functional (e.g., chain link) or decorative (e.g., split rail), depending on the task to be accomplished.

A gate can serve as either an invitation or a barrier. Give some thought to the type of entrance (and invitation) you want to provide. Figure 2.6 shows how a school in Boston has incorporated a signature gate into an existing chain link fence.

43

Figure 2.6 The act of stepping through this unique gate opening creates a personal sense of place and a feeling of adventure.

Maintenance and Logistical Considerations

"Be sure to stress that the custodian is one of the most important people in the whole process!"

—Teacher and land lab developer

Maintenance of an outdoor learning site is a critical element, but one that is often brushed aside or simply "assumed" as the excitement of planning the project builds. Maintenance and custodial staff are justifiably concerned about any changes that affect the appearance of the building or grounds. As you plan, include maintenance folks as a part of committees or planning sessions. Nothing creates more fear and animosity than being left out when others are planning changes to your turf. Invite custodial staff to be partners in the site enhancement process.

As feeding stations, brush piles, or unmowed areas are added to the site, it's important to consult with both administration and maintenance staff. That "perfect spot" that you have for a brush pile may interfere with mowing patterns or other plans for that area.

The big question, of course, is, "Will your great ideas make more work for me?" That's certainly a reasonable question considering that most maintenance folks already have more than enough work to do. It's unreasonable to expect custodians to also weed flower beds, fill bird feeders, and trim pathways. The bottom line: Outdoor upkeep and routine maintenance simply has to be done by volunteers.

Little things can help. For example, make sure that kids wipe feet well before tracking mud and dirt inside; be obsessive about squelching littering; invite the custodian to watch—or better yet, help with—an outdoor learning activity.

Getting the Help You Need

Once in place, many outdoor instructional features such as brush piles, seating, and unmowed areas need little maintenance. Garden plots, pathways, feeding stations and water sources, however, do need attention. Some teachers simply incorporate basic care of the site into the classroom routine. With tight teaching schedules, however, this is often not possible. Schools with after-school or summer programs can handle the maintenance of the land lab more easily since schedules for these programs may be more flexible.

If your school site enhancements are rather complex, you may want to consider approaching community groups for assistance. A local garden or service club, for example, may be willing to take on the weeding and care of a garden plot. A small sign in the garden acknowledging the help can go a long way toward cementing a beautiful relationship. Scout groups, 4-H clubs, or other youth groups may also be willing to take on a specific responsibility around the schoolyard including edging, trimming, or mulching. Try to give volunteer groups small but clearly defined tasks.

Using community help also can be a powerful public relations tool. As folks help maintain the school site, a feeling of ownership develops. Remember that many small clubs and organizations are often scrambling for speakers and programs for their meetings. Your offer to speak at a monthly meeting about the types of learning activities that take place on the site because of their generous help can make friends and solidify future support. Bringing along a few students to share their outdoor learning experiences is even better!

Schoolwide maintenance days can be another way to get many hands involved. The principal at one Ohio elementary school designates one day in both fall and spring as "land lab cleanup days." This school has garden space allocated to each grade level, so classes concentrate on their part of the site. The cleanup provides dual benefits: it focuses attention on the outdoor learning site and gets the garden back in good condition.

Litter Begets Litter

We could also add that graffiti begets graffiti. It's the old story—if litter is not removed, there is a high probability that more trash will be tossed. Trash receptacles need to be included on the school site and emptied before they overflow.

School custodians have long recognized the importance of removing graffiti as quickly as possible. As with litter, the longer that the offensive scrawl is visible, the greater the likelihood that more will appear. If graffiti is a recurring problem, you may want to investigate the many anti-graffiti coatings that are available commercially or plant vines to hide frequently attacked walls.

45

Vandalism Concerns

Unfortunately, vandalism is almost a universal problem. There is no way to "vandal proof" an outdoor area. But, there are some steps that can be taken to make the site somewhat vandal resistant:

- Place areas with benches and tables in view of the building.
- Mount signage on sturdy posts. If the sign is broken or defaced, the most difficult part to install is still in the ground.
- Consider security lighting for particularly vulnerable areas.
- Develop the site slowly; a massive overnight change in the school grounds attracts attention and sets up an appealing challenge to vandals. Projects and features that emerge over time are more likely to be viewed as just part of the landscape.
- Repair vandalized areas promptly. Replacing signs or plantings quickly has been shown to decrease future vandalism.

The most frequently mentioned antidote for minimizing schoolyard vandalism is student and community involvement as the area is developed. Involve many students from a variety of grade levels in the planning and establishment of elements on the school site. Encouraging neighborhood involvement on work days and special events is also very positive. The more people who have a positive interest in your project, the more eyes that will be watching your site. Stories abound of how vandalism was stopped or greatly reduced once the neighborhood was invited to view the space as theirs also.

If vandalism does occur, it should be treated as a crime and reported to the proper authorities. Letting students see that damaged property, including plantings, is viewed as a crime can be a valuable learning experience in itself.

Take heart, though. Vandalism, although a concern, does not usually occur regularly or in devastating proportions on a school outdoor study site. If you can develop a sense of school and community ownership, and also keep the site neat and in good repair, acts of vandalism should be only occasional annoyances.

Invasive Species

The use of plants native to your area is preferred for a variety of reasons. As you are using your outdoor classroom, however, it's very likely that you will encounter examples of invasive species on the site. Understanding the concept of invasive species and the concerns it raises can be a worthwhile learning experience for a class. Check out the National Park Service's "Weeds Gone Wild" website at http://www.nps.gov/plants/alien/index.htm for an excellent compilation of information and resources. To find out what plants are considered invasive in your area, search the Internet for "(your state) invasive species."

Storage and Water

Most teachers point out that an outdoor locked storage shed is a necessary component of the schoolyard site. It saves both enormous amounts of time and indoor storage space to have yard tools, feeder food, and even teaching resources located outside on the site. As you prepare a budget, be sure to include a locked storage shed on the list.

If you have garden plots, a water source is essential. Being able to connect a garden hose near the area to be watered is necessary if watering is to be done with any regularity. Carrying a sprinkling can for 100 yards gets old very quickly! If a water line can't be extended to the planting area, it might be best to move the plantings closer to the water spigot.

Gardens as Teaching Tools

Using school gardens as teaching tools is an idea that has been around since the early 1900s. School gardens were a reaction to the negative environmental consequences of urban industrialization. Gardens were seen as a way to provide children with exposure to nature that was being rapidly lost in highly populated cities. The school garden concept was very appealing, and by the early 1900s nearly every state had schools with gardens.

Garden plots give kids direct contact with nature and provide a wonderful living laboratory for exploring cycles in nature. Gardens can add to the aesthetics of a site as well as reinforcing concepts such as responsibility, patience, and stewardship.

Gardens are truly interdisciplinary and can be linked to the curriculum in many ways. The science concepts are obvious, but gardens can also build upon math concepts (e.g., measurement, estimation, data collection), language arts (e.g., journaling, creative writing), social studies (e.g., research concerning plants that were historically and economically important in the area), and art (e.g., nature as a subject for drawing or photography).

There are many books, articles, and Internet sites that provide detailed examples of garden designs. Several excellent examples of these are located in the references at the end of this book. If schoolyard gardening sounds appealing, you need to decide whether you want to have individual classroom gardens, or a larger group garden that may be tended by several classrooms or an entire school. Individual classroom gardens provide the greatest flexibility—you and your students decide what will be planted and how to care for it. It's very easy to assign tasks and monitor progress. As always, start small! You can always expand the plot next year.

Group gardens provide the opportunity to use a larger plot of land. As a result, crops requiring more space (e.g., pumpkins) can be easily planted. As with any group endeavor, there need to be clearly defined responsibilities for each of the participating classes. Some group gardens are really a patchwork of smaller plots, while others are large plots with tasks rotated among classes—one classroom waters, another weeds, while another maintains the individual plants.

47

Types of Gardens

There are as many types of gardens as there are garden developers! On a page compiled by Amanda Vanhoozier appearing on the Texas Cooperative Extension website (http://aggiehorticulture.tamu.edu/kinder/theme.html), school gardens are classified into three broad categories. These three ways of using gardens can help to answer the question, "What shall we plant?"

Concept Gardens

Broad concepts about plants and nature can be studied in a garden with a diversity of plants. The garden easily branches out into scientific and environmental studies, theories and principles. For example, plant life cycles, plant form and function, food production in plants, regeneration of plants, biodiversity, seasonal cycles or adaptation could all be studied.

Tips for Garden Plots

The University of California Cooperative Extension–San Diego has some excellent tips for garden plots. Here are a few excerpts from their very useful " school gardens" link from their website:

Be conservative: Gardens can quickly become too large. Start small and see what you can maintain. You can always expand the plot later.

Sketch it out: Make a diagram that shows garden plot areas, dimensions, walkways, water source, tool storage, and fencing or gate (if applicable). The garden should be placed in a convenient location. Most school gardens are placed near the building for easy access and water availability. Of course, avoid being too near play equipment or areas of high foot traffic.

Determine crops: You need to decide what types of plantings will be placed on the site. Pay careful attention to the growing season in your area, and to the types of plants that will be successful. Attention to harvesting and blooming dates, as well as proper row spacing and plant placement, are important factors.

Keep records and photos: Great idea! Planting records can be very useful and educational. Photos also provide a chance to document the types of plantings in the garden over the years and can create interest for incoming classes.

Consider water source, drainage, and sunlight: The garden should be in an area that has rather easy access to a water spigot. Watering and tool cleanup is so much easier if a water source is readily available. Avoid placing the garden in a low area where water collects. For best results, the garden should receive six to eight hours of sunlight per day.

Find good soil: The extension folks recommend developing your plot in areas that already have existing weed and grass growth. In addition, avoid areas that have been treated with herbicides. The soil should be workable—ideally crumbly, well aerated, able to hold water. (http://cesandiego.ucdavis.edu/School_Gardens/)

Topic Gardens

A specific topic can be investigated in a topic garden. Topics may include seeds (monocot or dicot), roots, soils, beneficial insects, leaves, drought-resistance, or flowers.

Theme Gardens

. . . These gardens incorporate an interdisciplinary approach to your garden. Your curriculum or class interests can give direction to your theme. (Vanhoozier)

Vanhoozier provides a list of wonderful examples including: an alphabet garden, native plant butterfly garden, sundial garden, herb/scent garden, prairie garden, Peter Rabbit's Garden.

Most school gardens seem to utilize a theme approach. Of course, concepts and topics can also be addressed in themed gardens. I'm always amazed at the many themes that people create. There are the old favorites, such as butterfly gardens, hummingbird gardens, herb gardens, vegetable gardens, and perennial gardens. But the possibilities for garden themes are limitless. Following are a few other great creative ideas that teachers have developed.

Pizza Garden

Include plants that might end up as pizza toppings (tomatoes, onions, peppers, and so on).

Shakespeare Garden

This could be any author. Include plants that are mentioned in the author's work.

Biblical Garden

Grow plants mentioned in the Bible.

Sensory Garden

Design this type of garden with plants that have distinctive appeal in terms of sight, sound, touch, smell, and even taste.

State-Themed Garden

Include plants that played an important part in your state history or economy.

49

School Name Garden

Use plants that represent the letters of your school's name.

Storybook Garden

Use plants that are associated with books that are class favorites.

Shape Garden

Use plants that have unusual leaf or flower shapes.

Multicultural Garden

Incorporate plants associated with different cultures.

Farm Crop Garden

Cultivate plants commonly grown on farms in your state.

State Flower Garden

Plant the state flowers of several states in your region of the country.

Fibonacci Garden

Plant flowers or other plants that contain a number from the Fibonacci sequence in either the flowers, seeds, or leaf structure (1, 2, 3, 5, 8, 13, 21 . . .).

Additional Thoughts About Gardens

Our culture associates the word *garden* with an area that is relatively well maintained. A garden gone wild will generate negative comments much more quickly than an unmowed area being used as a study site. Also, since gardens are usually close to the school building, the community frequently views them as part of the general landscaping. Bottom line: gardens need to be weeded and maintained.

In northern climates, gardens can be planted only late in the school year. As a result, blooming flowers and harvested crops may not be possible until the start of a new school year. Choose plants carefully in terms of blooming and ripening times. You don't want everything to reach its peak in July! Some teachers have kids plant spring flowering bulbs in the fall so that the plants will bloom while school is still in session.

Summer maintenance can be a concern. Some schools have parents sign up for summer gardening chores. In many cases, though, a thorough weeding right at the end of the school year followed by a weeding at the beginning of the school year is all that is really needed. The garden needn't be a summer showcase—just reasonably maintained. During dry spells, however, some provision should be made for volunteers to water.

Include the Birds

Of course, natural food sources can be augmented through the use of bird feeders. Entire books have been written, and websites abound, describing the almost limitless variety of feeder styles that can be made or purchased. Bird feeders can provide realistic opportunities for data collection while fostering feelings of responsibility and stewardship. Feeders placed near classroom windows can provide wonderful, up-close encounters with wildlife that can spark a lifelong interest in birding.

Project FeederWatch, sponsored by the Cornell Lab of Ornithology, is a fantastic program that gives students an opportunity to observe and record data about the birds that visit their feeders. Students can then choose composite data displays for their region, and see how their observations compared with others. Check out the website at http://www.birds.cornell.edu/pfw/.

The National Audubon Society is also an excellent resource. Their AUDUBON ADVENTURES is an environmental education program for grades 3–6 that utilizes resource kits including student nature news magazines and classroom resource and activity information. Audubon has also developed an exciting model for an after-school program designed for students in grades 6–8. The Audubon education web page can be found at: http://www.audubon.org/educate/.

Getting Started

If you are excited about the idea of establishing some outdoor learning locations on your school site, share your enthusiasm with another person! Schoolyard-enhancement efforts are much more doable and have greater staying power if more than one teacher is involved. As you begin to work on your project, keep the following items in mind.

51

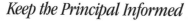

Keep the Principal Informed

This has to be the first step! Any outdoor enhancement project, even on a small scale, needs to be understood and backed by your school administration. Although your plans may be in the very early formation stage, bounce your ideas off the principal. As planning continues, keep the principal in the loop through informal chats as well as membership on planning committees. In a very real sense, your project won't go anywhere unless it has the support of the principal.

Planning Groups

If your project is small scale, you may not need a formal planning committee beyond the students in your classroom. On the other hand, if you want to encourage wider usage of the school grounds and plan to add a variety of outdoor habitat features, it is essential to involve a mix of folks in the planning. Some examples of possible categories for membership include:

- grade-level representatives
- maintenance staff
- art, music, and physical education teachers
- teachers of special education classes
- parents and neighbors
- students
- administrative representatives
- local business representatives
- community agencies or organizations that might have an interest in the site
- technical advisors (naturalists, scientists, experienced land lab developers, and so on)

The size and composition of your planning committee reflect the scope of your project. A basic rule of thumb for setting up a planning committee is to include representatives from all constituencies that will be either utilizing or affected by the project, as well as persons with special expertise. It's a good idea to err on the side of having too many folks on the committee rather than risk overlooking a category. Broad-based planning committees can be a bit cumbersome. But, in the bigger picture, a varied committee develops a sense of ownership and pride in the site, and also can lead you to resources that you would never have found on your own.

Site Inventory

The term *site inventory* sounds impressive, but it actually is just a listing or mapping of the types of natural features that are already on your schoolyard site. A site inventory is especially useful if your site includes wooded or overgrown areas, since notable habitats and plant species can easily be overlooked by the untrained eye.

Invite a naturalist to walk the site with you. Take along a GPS device and a camera to record locations of interesting natural features so that they can readily be found again. Many organizations and government agencies have people well versed in botany and zoology who are very willing to share their expertise. These include professionals from:

- nature centers
- soil and water conservation district offices (SWCD)
- cooperative extension offices
- state department of natural resources (DNR) staff
- college or university science faculty

State and federal agencies that focus on natural resources usually have education specialists who are delighted to help with the development of a school site. It's definitely worth your time to have a professional look at the school site early in the planning process and point out where features should be located to maximize the resources that you already have.

Finding Funding for Outdoor Projects

Great ideas, but not enough money? Welcome—you are not alone! The good news is that unless you are planning to implement a very large schoolyard-enhancement program, the expenses do not have to be great. The bigger expenses usually are from benches, work surfaces, signage, storage sheds, and pathway material. As is true in life, on most items you can spend a lot or a little. Is the 400-dollar bench critical to meeting your objectives, or will the 100-dollar model work?

Keep in mind that everything doesn't have to be done at once. If cash is tight, prioritize the most essential items and postpone others. Enhancements to attract wildlife like feeding stations, brush piles, small garden plots, and unmowed areas cost almost nothing but quickly engage the interest of students and teachers.

53

Look Locally

I have found that most teachers have had the greatest success with local benevolence. Many communities have foundations or family trust funds that prefer to make small grants (usually under 10,000 dollars). These local sources are much more likely to give you money than a national funder and often have a simpler application process. The downside can be time. Often, small trust funds meet only a few times a year to make awards.

Finding these local trust funds and foundations can be a little tricky, though, since most are not listed in the phone book. Contact tax-exempt agencies or the development office of a local college or university. Explain your project and ask if they know of any local trusts or foundations that might fund projects like yours. Usually, development folks are very helpful and willing to steer you in a fruitful direction (as long as they aren't working on a similar project!).

Agency Grants

Frequently, state and federal agencies have grant funds available. Usually, these are for specific items or projects (e.g., purchasing items made from recycled materials or planting tree seedlings). It can be difficult to know who has what type of grant or resource available. One of the best ways to find out is to contact a nature center, soil and water conservation district office, cooperative extension service, or state department of natural resources office. These folks usually have a good handle on the types of money flowing from government agencies.

Local Businesses

Consider both hometown firms as well as the "big box" stores. Business usually will be more likely to donate merchandise rather than money to a project. One elementary school asked for "some" potting soil and was both surprised and delighted to see a large, fully loaded truck pull up to the school!

Many of the large, national chain stores include local grant giving as corporate policy. Check the websites of these stores or, better yet, contact the store manager to see if local grants are available.

Parents

In many ways, parents are probably your best source of getting the help and materials you need. The diversity of occupations and contacts that are represented by the parents of your students can be very useful. Often a parent may have a friend or relative who can also provide help, materials, or even funding tips.

Parents can also be very helpful when it comes to getting equipment or machinery that is needed to work on the site. Renting a skid loader or auger can be expensive, but chances are that in a classroom of twenty-five, someone's parent has the connections you need!

Keeping It Going

What Happened in Georgia

The Georgia Wildlife Federation was justifiably concerned. From 1989–2003, there had been more than 2,000 outdoor classroom projects in the state requesting certification or funding. However, a 2004 research study conducted by the Federation to follow up on school projects produced a disturbing statistic—more than forty percent of the responding random sample schools no longer had active outdoor programs! (2005, 6)

Listed among the top reasons for the failure of outdoor classrooms were:

- continued maintenance and upkeep
- teachers unsure or unable to incorporate usage into lessons

These are important concerns to keep in mind. Too often, enhancements are added to a school site because they "look nice" or "might be useful." Whether it's a bird feeder or a seating area, there is always some upkeep that is needed. To justify the extra effort, only enhancements that can be directly related to the required curriculum should be added, at least initially. As enhancements are being planned and added to the school site, teachers also need to be provided with information, activity suggestions, and even inservice opportunities to help clarify how site enhancements can be effectively incorporated into teaching.

I also have seen wonderful outdoor teaching facilities fall into disarray and eventual disuse after just a few years. It's almost inconceivable that a project that began with such energy could just wither on the proverbial vine. Usually one or both of the following reasons contribute to the problem.

Too Big Too Soon

One simple phrase that teachers have said to me over and over again is, "start small." That's easy to say but hard to do, especially when you have a group of enthusiastic people generating all kinds of wonderful ideas for enhancing the school site. It's fine to dream big and capture a vision for what you would like your school site to become, but try to steer your planning group into also developing a realistic time line for the next two or three years.

Overly ambitious projects drain the energy and enthusiasm of volunteers. It's also often difficult to gauge the time required for maintenance or upkeep of certain features such as school garden plots, feeding stations, or trails. Begin by creating an element that can be used by a variety of classes. An excellent starting point is to focus energy first on the creation of an outdoor teaching/meeting area. That creates an outdoor focal point and also helps teachers to visualize how a class can be managed outdoors.

Only One Person's Dream

If a schoolyard site is to be maintained effectively, it must be more than one person's pet project. Projects that are driven by the efforts and personalities of only one or two people usually do not last for more than a few years. The original developers may move, retire, or just tire out!

The Georgia study also lists some reasons why outdoor classrooms succeed, with community support and student involvement ranking high on the list. I am assuming that the term *community* is being used broadly to include the school faculty and staff as well as the residents living near the school.

If you are one of the catalysts behind a school-site habitat project, try to involve a lot of other staff members. As with any change, you need to show other teachers how the efforts to use the outdoors as a tool can make instruction more meaningful. You can also build a sense of ownership by having different classrooms in charge of maintaining specific areas on the site. Some groups keep feeders filled, others keep the water sources fresh, and another class weeds the butterfly garden periodically. If students are involved in planning and maintaining the site, their enthusiasm and energy will encourage adults to keep the project going.

If the school site enhancements require significant maintenance (e.g., gardens or trails), go into the community and seek help from clubs, youth groups, and other organizations. Your time may be better spent in establishing a community support network for what you have, rather than adding some new features to the site.

To Put Things in Perspective

This chapter contains a bundle of specific suggestions and possibilities for enhancing a school site. We've mentioned everything from sun shelters and benches to garden plots and decorative entrances. Although my goal is to provide a variety of ideas and options, it's critical to remember that schoolyard-enhanced learning is not driven by materials and building projects.

Powerful learning experiences await you just beyond the classroom door. Kids carrying sit-upons and clipboards can experience the wonder of nature by exploring the plants and critters in an unmowed area of the playground. It's great if you have special seating areas, formal trails, raised gardens, or professional-looking signage, but these are by no means essential. Schoolyard-enhanced learning happens when you and the kids step outside for instruction. It's not defined by equipment or landscaping.

57

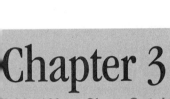

Chapter 3

Taking Your Class Outside: The Nuts and Bolts

The principal was definitely skeptical. Small groups of fifth graders were energetically releasing balloons on the playground and then running to mark the landing spots with hula hoops. Although she viewed herself as a progressive educator, she couldn't help but question how this would relate to learning. Walking closer, she saw that pairs of children were using a plant identification chart they had made to see whether four specific species of plants were in the sample area marked by the hula hoops. After several samplings, the students went inside and discussed what type of chart or graph to draw that would best communicate their findings. As the process unfolded, any doubts about the value of the activity quickly evaporated!

Taking students outdoors does make for a great change of pace and place, but effective outdoor learning requires more than just a walk outside. This chapter focuses on practical and specific tips and tricks for incorporating the outdoors as a powerful learning tool. The chapter is organized around some very realistic concerns and questions that teachers frequently voice as they consider using the outdoors as a tool:

- How can I create and maintain support for outdoor teaching?
- How can I provide a safe outdoor experience?

- What should I first do indoors to ensure a good experience outdoors?
- How can I teach most effectively and efficiently outdoors?
- What are some ways to build on outdoor experiences back in the classroom?

Getting the Support You Need

Schoolyard-enhanced learning needs the support of administrators, colleagues, and parents. If things are to go smoothly, especially over the long haul, all three groups need to understand why you are using this nontraditional instructional method. Once the benefits are understood, the support will follow.

Administrators

Although more and more educators and parents are recognizing the value of moving beyond the four walls of the classroom, we can't assume that everyone understands the concept of outdoor enhanced learning. It is especially important that your principal understand the rationale so that you have a knowledgeable advocate for outdoor learning ready to greet parents in the front office. Since administrators are usually the first to be contacted by a parent, it is critical that they understand both the "what" and the "why" of schoolyard-enhanced learning.

Invite Your Principal to Join You

Seeing an activity is more powerful than hearing it explained or reading a brief account in a lesson plan. The balloons and hula hoops instantly made sense when the principal actually saw the project in action. Invite your principal to join your class outside and encourage your students to explain what they are doing and why it's helpful to be outdoors.

It's reassuring for a principal to be able to address a questioning parent by saying, "When I was with the class outside yesterday . . ." Administrators are much more comfortable fielding questions when they have actually participated in a program or activity.

Connect to Required Standards or Content

Since most states have academic content standards of some type, it is crucial that administrators clearly and quickly see how outdoor

60

instruction is linked to those standards. The days of justifying a method by saying, "This is good for kids—look how much they are enjoying the experience," are gone. Mandated curriculum and standards-based testing have made it essential that there be clear linkages between activities and standards.

The great news is that outdoor learning experiences can be clearly linked to standards-based requirements. It's essential, though, that administrators be well informed as to how the standards are incorporated into outdoor instruction. The most effective way to do that is to provide your principal with a brief, written overview of your activity that shows specific links to the curriculum. I have been amazed how many critics are silenced when they see that the curriculum is linked directly to the outdoor activity. After a while, it is not as important to document every lesson in advance. But, in the early stages, it's best to leave no doubt that the outdoor experience is embedded in the curriculum.

61

Colleagues

Spread the Enthusiasm

Your strongest source of support may be next door or right across the hall. Every teacher whom I interviewed emphasized the importance of working with colleagues as you develop outdoor activities or add enhancements to the school site. You don't need schoolwide participation, but it does help to have at least one other person who is willing to give outdoor instruction a try. Energy and creativity are wonderful by-products when two or three teachers share enthusiasm about a new approach or activity.

Fifth-grade teacher Linda Lang has had great success working on a project with a kindergarten teacher in her building. Linda teaches a bird unit in science and pairs up her fifth graders with kindergarten students. She calls the pairs "birding buddies." After studying about birds, the older students do neat activities with the younger ones. Interestingly, there are virtually no discipline problems as the pairs are working together. The older students seem very intent on nurturing the younger ones.

Share Resources

Whenever possible, try to locate classroom sets of equipment or other resources so that they can be shared by everyone. For example, sets of hand lenses, binoculars, or GPS units purchased by a parent group or through small grants can be housed in the media center for checkout by any classroom. To entice people to use the equipment, include some sample activities in the equipment box.

I don't know anyone who was ever "talked into" using the outdoors for instruction. In most cases, teachers saw a colleague enthusiastically using the schoolyard and decided to give it a try also. Frequently, there are several teachers on a staff who are genuinely interested in making use of the outdoors but need to see someone modeling some examples of how it can be done. It's the old story—enthusiasm is infectious!

Parents

Involve Parents and Community

Administrators are grateful for parents who are enthusiastic advocates of the school. Getting parents involved with projects to maintain school gardens or enhance the school site with projects such as those described in Chapter 2 has several positive results. First, parents can point with satisfaction to their own efforts. Also, as the parents help, there is a wonderful opportunity for us to explain how these features are used for instruction. Finally, parents who have a sense of ownership combined with an understanding of the educational value of the school site become enthusiastic advocates for the school and its willingness to provide unique learning opportunities.

Following are some of the numerous ways parents can help.

Skills and Labor

Many of the site enhancements described in Chapter 2, such as equipment or teaching materials, can be made or moved to the site by parents. Bird feeders, benches, or work surfaces can be great projects for parents with carpentry skills. Locating and moving logs or boulders also are ideal parent projects.

Contacts in the Community

Whether you need wood or paint, gravel or signage, a parent or relative can help obtain free materials. Someone probably works at a place that has just what you need. Often an employee is much more likely to get the donation than you would be.

Locating and Writing Grants

One teacher in central Ohio needed a small grant to fund a storage shed and some basic equipment for a school garden. Since she and her class were very busy preparing and planting the garden, there just was no possibility of doing the time-consuming task of hunting for grant opportunities in the community. After the teacher casually mentioned the need at a school open house, a parent volunteered to look for grants. Amazingly this parent was able to find enough grant money to fund a larger storage shed and twice the amount of equipment than was first proposed.

Knowledge and Enthusiasm

It doesn't matter if the parent is a professional botanist or a weekend angler; both may provide a wealth of outdoor knowledge and nature lore. I have often found that the amateur outdoor enthusiast brings along an energy that kids really love. There's nothing like someone's grandma excitedly talking about her pet black rat snake as it clings to her arm!

Extra Supervision

Not only do you get extra help when taking students outside, but parents get to see firsthand what this outdoor teaching stuff is all about. It's truly a win-win situation.

Outdoor Equipment and Supplies

It's amazing how many bird feeders, clipboards, and old pairs of binoculars are languishing in garages and basements. You can also save a lot of money if basic items such as wood, paint, and brushes are donated instead of purchased.

Assistance During the Summer Months

Parents can be especially helpful during the summer months when the students are gone but the weeds keep growing! Some schools have sign-up sheets for families to commit to donating a half day to weed the school gardens or keep a trail trimmed back.

One family of three took great pride in weeding a small flower bed near the school entrance every week. It became a time for the parents and child to work together on a project that drew them together and also helped the school. Keeping parents involved is not only enjoyable for the family, but also develops a very powerful feeling of ownership in the school site.

Link with Community Groups

Community service groups such as garden clubs or scout troops are often looking for projects. They frequently welcome the opportunity to partner with the school to enhance the school grounds. Scout troops, for example, can provide the people power and energy that can get a time-consuming and potentially expensive project done quickly.

At my son's high school, a trail had been cut through a wooded area adjoining the school, but there was no signage, marked points of interest, or trail map. Mike was beginning to work on an Eagle Scout project and saw the trail as a potential community service project. He worked with the teacher to mark points of biological interest, drew a detailed trail map, designed sign posts for points of interest, brought in a group of scouts to dig and cement heavy-duty identification markers, and even put together an activity guide for other teachers who might want to use the trail.

A task of this magnitude would have been a time-consuming challenge for one teacher to accomplish during the school year. However, by tapping the resources of the local scout troop, a valuable learning area was enhanced in a relatively short span of time.

Keep Parents in the Loop

It is only natural for parents to wonder why you are taking their children outside. If the educational benefits are explained, however, most parents will support outdoor enhanced learning.

One teacher made a video of students doing activities outside. The kids narrated the video themselves, explaining the content connections. The DVD plays during open houses and parent-teacher conference times. Parents enjoy seeing their children and also leave with a better understanding of how the outdoors can enhance learning. Once parents understand that outdoor activities are linked to the curriculum, and that safety concerns have been addressed, they usually become enthusiastic supporters.

Take advantage of classroom newsletters, school websites, open houses, and informational handouts to let parents know that your classroom will include more than the four walls. Briefly describe the types of activities that you plan to do outside and show how the outdoor experiences clearly relate to the curriculum. Emphasize how outdoor-enhanced learning helps to:

- make the abstract more concrete
- build on a natural curiosity about the outdoors
- provide active learning experiences
- provide a change of pace and place that makes learning more meaningful

Safety First

Keeping children safe has to be our main concern, whether we are inside or out. As teachers, we usually have pretty accurate "gut feelings" when it comes to student safety. You have a good knowledge of your community, the neighborhood around the school, and the features that make up your schoolyard. As you draw on that knowledge base, here are a few basic tips that teachers frequently emphasize.

Keeping Parents Informed Via the Web

Eighth-grade teacher Josh Flory makes maximum use of his school web page to inform parents about his use of the outdoors for instruction. By visiting his web page at http://curriculum.new-albany.k12.oh.us/jflory/specialprojects.htm, you can see how he provides parents with information about the "sit area" activity that is described in Chapter 5. Note how this concise page explains the activity and also provides a rationale for outdoor learning:

- an article to access that talks about the importance of exposing students to nature
- background about the "sit area" activity
- an explanation of purpose

When the "sit area" activity is under way, Josh will often include a download site so that parents can see a map of where the students are working, as well as examples of student reflections about what they have learned.

65

Let the Office Know When You Are Going Outside

Few things are more embarrassing to an administrator than to walk into a classroom with a parent only to find the room empty and no clue where the class might be. At the very least, write a note on the board letting people know where you are. It may seem like a small matter, but unfortunately, I have seen knee-jerk reactions to such situations that have put an end to outdoor teaching at a building.

Take Along a Cell Phone

Cell phones can be annoying, but they can also save the day in an emergency situation. Here's another option—discount stores sell very inexpensive walkie-talkie units that can give you instant communication with the school office or another teacher in the building.

Be Aware of Allergies and Other Special Needs

The medical concerns of your students will most certainly govern the types of activities you can do in any given school year. In a year when you have several children with asthma or severe bee sting reactions, you will probably do outdoor activities of much shorter duration and in closer proximity to the building than in other years.

A child's Individualized Educational Plan (IEP) certainly plays a major role in determining feasible outdoor activities. Teaming with a special education teacher for outdoor activities can provide a rich experience for everyone. There is a growing body of research that shows that many children with special needs can benefit tremendously from outdoor learning experiences.

Show Kids Poison Ivy and Other Natural Hazards

I am continually amazed how many children (and adults!) are not able to recognize poison ivy. If I am going to be outside in an area where this plant grows, one of my first teaching stops is beside a poison ivy plant like the one in Figure 3.1.

I usually have to counter the inevitable response from the child who says, "I never get it." It is very common for people to seem immune at one time, but then develop the rash after another exposure. Emphasize that this is one plant that is absolutely off limits! Of course, also explain how the berries from this plant are very beneficial to birds and other animals.

Figure 3.1 Although this specimen is a climbing vine, poison ivy can be found as a shrub and as ground cover. Be sure students know how to spot noxious plants in your area.

In areas of the country where poisonous snakes can be found, the National Wildlife Federation recommends that leaders or participants always turn a rock or log toward themselves, grasping the edge of the object farthest from where they are standing. That provides a safe escape route for a startled animal (2004).

Especially in early fall, be on the lookout for yellow-jacket colonies. Take a few minutes to scan the area to see if any stinging critters seem to be flying toward the same location. If so, stay far away!

Give the "Don't Put Stuff in Your Mouth" Talk

One warm spring day I was doing an activity with a group of sixth graders in which we passed around a rock and used adjectives to describe it. The student next to me was the last to handle the rock. Of course, many of the words he had planned to use had been taken already. Out of frustration (and just a little impishness!) he impulsively licked the rock and said "It tastes salty." Good observation, but a bad idea—he had just licked the accumulated perspiration of his classmates!

It's interesting how preschoolers to high schoolers will try to taste things they find outdoors. Although it should be obvious, especially for older students, it is still important to emphasize that items found outside should not be tasted.

Any teaching about edible plants in the wild needs to be handled very carefully and should only be done by a thoroughly trained and experienced naturalist. Dangerous plants often resemble edible plants to the untrained eye. I feel that teaching about edible plants should be a topic saved for adult audiences.

Take Another Adult on Extended Outings

A short trek to the schoolyard can often be easily done by one teacher. For longer excursions, or if the activity requires that you go to a far corner of a large school site, by all means, take along another adult and a basic first-aid kit.

There is no simple formula for how many adults should accompany a group outside. Ages of the students, complexity of the activity, length of the outdoor stay, and previous outdoor experience of the class all contribute to a decision regarding how much supervision is needed. As we know, classes have personalities! Some years a group may need only basic supervision, while another year the same activity would not be possible without additional help.

Before You Go Outside

It was a beautiful spring day. I was excited about taking my group of first graders outside to do a nature art activity. We were going to do "squish art" in which they used dirt, stones, leaves—anything that might leave a mark on paper—from a pasture field to color in a line drawing of either a frog or butterfly. Adjoining the school grounds was a farm field that we had permission to use.

I liked to use this area because it was a grazed pasture and had a wonderful diversity of plants (a.k.a. weeds!) that were perfect for this natural colors activity. You can imagine the look on my face when I trooped outside with my exuberant band of nature artists only to find the area recently plowed with not a plant to be seen! Fortunately, the activity was salvaged by using the school lawn as our plant source, but the experience reinforced for me the importance of scouting a teaching area in advance!

How Much Time?

Of course, there is no exact formula for the optimal length of an outdoor activity. I have found, though, that it's best to start with brief treks. If students have not regularly used the outdoors as a classroom, or if it's early in the school year, it's best to start with short excursions (fifteen to twenty minutes or so). These initial outdoor visits need to be very focused, usually accomplishing only one or two specific activities, such as:

"We are going to look for five examples of weathering."

"We are going to measure the flagpole without using a tape measure."

"Other than the school building, see if you can list five examples outside that show the impact of people on the natural environment."

It's ideal to begin your brief outdoor excursions early in the school year. Students quickly learn that the outdoors is simply an extension of your classroom. After some short trips outdoors, the activities can become more complex and the time outside can be extended.

When to Go Out?

More important than the time spent on an activity is the pattern of outdoor use. Kristin Metz of the Boston Schoolyard Initiative feels that students should go outside on a regular basis. She advises establishing a routine for using the outdoors, perhaps by designating a set day of the week for outdoor instructional activities.

And don't limit going outside only to those warm days in September or May! If you live in a cold climate, winter can be an especially rewarding time to do brief outdoor activities. A walk in the snow on a clear, cold winter day can provide an entirely different perspective and experience. Signs of animal life are often easier to see in winter than in the warmer months, and the senses just seem sharper on a brisk January day. It's important for kids to see that nature is interesting, varied, and accessible in all seasons of the year.

How frequently you go outside will vary greatly depending upon your location, weather, teaching objectives, and unexpected opportunities. The teachers I have interviewed suggest using the outdoors no less than once every month, with much greater usage during the warm months.

Keep in mind that "going outside" does not have to mean a time-consuming and schedule-altering extravaganza. Just quickly stepping outside to look for examples of geometric shapes in nature in the schoolyard certainly qualifies as outdoor instruction. Frankly, a pattern of doing frequent forty-minute outdoor activities is often more effective than the random half-day "big lesson."

Avoiding a "Recess" Mind-Set

For students of any age, going outside implies freedom, movement, and even different behavior expectations. We want students to feel relaxed in the outdoors, but it is critical that outdoor instruction not be equated with play time.

While still inside the classroom, it's essential to review the behaviors and rules that you expect outside. Clearly establish the location in which you will be working—the boundaries of your activity area need to be easily understood. Emphasize that many of the rules that apply indoors will also apply outside. Once you are outside, go over the rules again!

A signal for getting everyone's attention outdoors is also very useful. A whistle, small bell, even a bird call can be effective. When kids are spread out over an outdoor area, you want to be able to get their attention without having to yell.

Survey the Site

Even when using your own school grounds, it's always a good idea to walk the area you will be using at least a day before going outside. Maintenance work, storm damage, or unexpected litter and vandalism all can interfere with your planned activity (including unexpected plowing!).

When taking students off site to a park or nature preserve, the need to do a previsit shortly before the outing is absolutely essential. The trails you were planning to use may be closed or overgrown, restroom facilities may not be up to your expectations, parking areas may be closed or placed in different locations, or litter and pollution

69

may have made the location unsuitable. The time spent in a previsit to an off-site location is well worth the effort.

Use Outdoor Time for Doing, Not Telling

Whenever possible, use the indoors to take care of routine tasks. The following are items that, when managed indoors, will allow for more learning outdoors.

Arrange Work Groups

It's easier to assign activity partners and tasks while in the classroom. Kids are accustomed to your managing those types of details as a part of the regular indoor classroom routine. Keep in mind that many cooperative learning activities such as "think-pair-share" and "jigsaw" can be adapted for outside use also. For a jigsaw activity, set up the "home" and "expert" groups indoors, and give an overview of the task (e.g., exploring preassigned mini-habitats) before going outside. The expert groups can even begin to develop a plan for approaching the activity while still in the classroom.

Define Vocabulary and Provide Background Information

Since you will usually be going outside to reinforce concepts that have been introduced in the classroom, it's helpful to review the pertinent vocabulary and content objectives right before you move outside. A quick review of the concept being taught is often more efficiently done indoors where you have immediate access to visuals and a writing surface.

Provide an Overview of What Will Be Done Outside

To maximize instructional time outside, students need to understand very clearly what specific tasks are to be accomplished there. It's time well spent to explain activities inside and again outside. The indoor explanation sets the stage and also makes very clear that you have a definite purpose in mind for going outdoors.

Review Your Rules for Working Outdoors

Especially early in the school year, the rules for outdoor behavior need to be repeated frequently. Going over outdoor rules while still inside helps to underscore their importance. Since there are fewer distractions, classes tend to be more attentive indoors as you initially explain your expectations. Be sure, though, to review the rules and procedures again as soon as you are outside—the excitement of being outdoors can lead to momentary memory lapses!

Sort Equipment or Materials

Use indoor time to sort the equipment and materials needed and to place items in easily accessible containers. While indoors, divide up the responsibility for carrying, managing, and returning the various items.

Time outdoors is valuable and usually quite limited. Try not to spend outdoor time doing things you could do just as easily, and sometimes more effectively, inside.

Do You Have Everything You Need?

Before going out, double- and triple-check to make sure that you have all of the necessary materials and equipment. Unfortunately, I can remember too many instances when I have wasted precious outdoor time sending runners back to the classroom to bring out forgotten items. As the group waits outside, the possibility of behavior problems increases geometrically!

My own informal poll of items most frequently forgotten includes:

- pencils
- lapboards or clipboards
- hand wipes or paper towels
- small magnifiers
- small containers for specimens
- trash bags (to sit on when the grass is wet)
- pretrip bathroom breaks!

Storing materials for individual activities in clear, plastic, gallon freezer bags can make it easy to check if everything is there. The bags save space, display the contents, and keep your materials dry and organized.

When You Are Outside

You've planned the activity, explained necessary background information, reviewed the behavior expectations, and double-checked your materials and equipment. The final step is to open the door and move the crew outside. Although outdoor teaching isn't really much different than indoor teaching, here are a few practical tips that can help to make the experience flow smoothly.

How Far Is Too Far?

Clearly indicate boundaries. Telling students to "stay on this side of the sidewalk" is much clearer than saying, "Don't go too far." Some teachers tie ribbons or colorful string on trees and plants that they want to use as boundaries. I have even stuck long pieces of masking tape on objects to identify the limits of a study area.

Most outdoor activities don't require large amounts of space. Without clear boundaries, though, groups will radiate in all directions, causing time-consuming (and potentially dangerous) situations. As a general rule, I try to confine outdoor activities to the smallest area possible. It takes a long time to gather kids in from a wide area for discussion or sharing of findings. With everyone in close, it also is easier to give directions or modify an activity without having to run all over the grounds.

The Power of a Circle

Talking to students outdoors requires a little change of approach. I've found that a circle is the most effective way to give directions or debrief activities outdoors. You can have kids either stand or sit, but be sure that everyone is part of a tight circle, with no one lingering on the outside (see Figure 3.2). If there is bright sunlight, you may have to modify the circle so that students aren't squinting.

The circle conveys a sense of purposefulness and also fosters the feeling that we are a part of something special. In a very practical sense, it also makes it possible for you to quickly see everyone and monitor what's happening. Trying to talk to a mass of kids standing three or four deep just doesn't work. The first layer may be engaged, but it's anyone's guess beyond that!

Figure 3.2 Whether sitting or standing, a circle is the most effective way to focus student attention in an outdoor setting.

Circulate Constantly

Because the outdoors is loaded with natural distractions, it is important to frequently move around to all groups to monitor and refocus attention to the task. Kids like to share neat things that they have found. Also, they frequently need to have the task clarified or restated.

When it fits the activity, I try to have students work in pairs. Students actually seem more focused outside when they work in pairs rather than alone. Trios don't seem to work as well, and groups of four or more can become too large for everyone to stay involved.

Encourage Respect for Nature

Even a quick schoolyard outing should include reminders to respect all living things. Yep, that includes weeds, bugs and critters, and even fungi! Emphasize that all natural items that are found or used in an activity should be returned back to nature. If a rock or log is turned over, it should be carefully put back in its original place. Even small items such as sticks and stones should be left outdoors and not dumped in a trash can after an activity.

73

View the Unexpected as a Bonus

That fantastic toad that a student found may not have been in your lesson plan, but it can be a great springboard for discussing protective coloration! What a great way to make an abstract concept more concrete.

When outdoors, view the unexpected as a bonus, not an annoyance. Without a doubt, teaching outdoors is a bit more time-consuming than teaching indoors. The long-lasting impact, however, is worth every minute of extra time.

Moving Materials

Put your materials in a backpack rather than a box. Even inexpensive backpacks are loaded with pockets and compartments of various sizes to store equipment and materials. Leave standard items such as magnifiers, plastic freezer bags, and lapboards in the pack and they are always ready to go. No need to waste time hunting through a jumble of items piled in a box!

A Place to Sit and Write

Frequently, outdoor activities involve gathering data or recording observations while outside. Here are some inexpensive ways to make a classroom set of seating and writing materials that will fit in a backpack.

If students will need to write or record data, consider making simple lapboards. The simplest option is to purchase the type of manila folder that is enclosed on three sides to form a pocket. Add binder clips or large paper clips to hold papers. The pocket feature provides a great storage place for pencils or other small materials and papers. If you plan to be outside on dewy mornings, you can laminate the folders twice and leave a little edge of plastic film around the edges to improve moisture resistance. You now have an inexpensive set of lightweight, flat, and very portable writing surfaces. The light color also serves as a handy background for looking at specimens.

Often it's better to have students sitting on the ground rather than standing. Trash bags can make inexpensive and very portable sit-upons to use when the ground is damp with morning dew.

Noise Pollution

Listen for the mowers! I've had some great activities squelched by the unexpected appearance of a lawn mower or construction noise. Try to move the activity to a quieter area rather than wait for the sound to pass.

What Was That?

Bring along a few field guides. Often, kids are interested in learning the names of things they find. Standard naturalist field guides that reference a large geographic area can be overwhelming in their size and complexity. As an alternative, some teachers have students find pictures of local plants and animals and then make their own mini field guides. Your local Soil Conservation Service or Department of Natural Resources office can usually supply the pictures needed to assemble a chart of common local species. If something unusual turns up, you can always go to the commercial guide, but students enjoy finding the plant or animal in a guide they have made themselves. It's a powerful learning experience for a child to be able to locate a found item in a guide and then be able to say with authority what it is!

There are some excellent field guides designed for children. The National Audubon Society has produced a wonderful series of First Field Guides designed specifically for children ages eight years and older. The books focus on the fifty most easily found species and make stunning use of full color pictures. There are a dozen books in the series ranging from amphibians to wildflowers (and, of course, birds!).

To Gather or Not to Gather

This opens the proverbial can of worms! On the one hand, we want children to experience nature and observe it closely. That type of observation is sometimes best done by collecting a natural item for closer inspection. On the other hand, it is vitally important that we teach children a respect for the natural world, and strongly discourage the random destruction of plants and habitats as well as the unnecessary removal of natural materials from a location.

If you are on a field trip to a state or national park (and many private or municipal parks), the answer is quite simple: You are not permitted to remove materials from these locations. If you are a guest on private land, common courtesy requires that you explain what you plan to do and ask permission to collect.

Whether to collect on the school grounds presents a different situation. Of course, if the plant can be studied where it is, don't disturb it. The National Wildlife Federation promotes the "1-in-20" rule for collecting common plants.

Collect a plant only if more than 20 of the same species are growing in your immediate area. If 20 plants are growing in an area, collect only one; if there are 40, collect only 2 and so on. This applies to parts of plants as well: remove one leaf off a shrub with 20 leaves; 1 fern from a clump of 20, etc. (2004)

Lists of local endangered species are available from your state department of natural resources. It can make for a good indoor lesson to have kids locate pictures of these species either on the Internet or in field guides. Your odds of finding these may be very small, especially on the school grounds. But, by making children aware of endangered species in their own locality, they become better-informed users of the outdoors.

Collecting animal specimens on the school grounds opens a variety of ethical and safety concerns. The "Resources" section at the

75

end of this book provides a variety of useful references that give very specific guidance concerning the care of live animals in the classroom. In most cases, it's just not a good idea to bring wild critters—even small ones—into the classroom, especially in the elementary grades. Wildlife of any size needs very special care to survive in an indoor environment. Unless we are willing to do careful research about an animal and can give the time and resources needed to keep wildlife humanely in an indoor environment, critters are best studied outside.

Inside the Building Again

When you are in Sue Cook's sixth-grade classroom, you are not sure whether you are indoors or out! The shelves have everything from seed pods to snake skins. The bookshelves are loaded with nature books and outdoor-related posters are everywhere. At the back of the room is a child's wading pool that has been converted to simulate a pond. On the table is an aquarium with a black rat snake dozing in the warmth of the afternoon.

As Sue teaches, she refers frequently to the natural teaching aids that fill her room. The topic today is habitats and she uses the mini-pond to illustrate the factors that are essential for life. She then has her students refer to the notes they took concerning the plants and animals that they found while doing the schoolyard survey yesterday.

Outdoor learning activities need to be thoroughly integrated into the general instructional routine. Students should clearly see how the treks outdoors mesh with the indoor instructional program. They also need opportunities to share and reflect about their experiences outside.

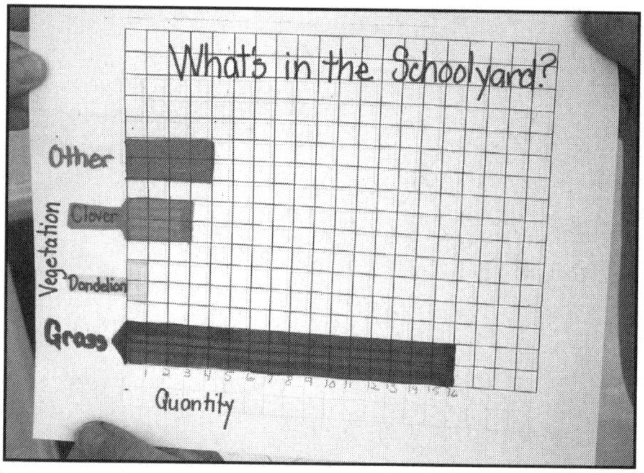

Using What You Found Outdoors

The outdoors can be a wonderful data source. There are items to count, changes to note, patterns to record, and observations to log.

Use the data and observations to help you teach content indoors. For a math unit on charts and graphs, use data found outside as your raw material for graphing. For examples, see Figure 3.3. Use outdoor observations

Figure 3.3 The Balloon Launch activity described in Chapter 5 provided the data for producing this bar graph.

to fuel a creative writing lesson or incorporate shapes and patterns observed in nature into artistic expressions.

Monitoring an outdoor area throughout the year can yield great opportunities for indoor discussions of concepts such as patterns and change. Eighth-grade teacher Josh Flory has his students identify a "sit area," a small, defined space outside that students return to repeatedly during the year and make detailed observations. Indoors, students are asked to write about what they observed and learned by concentrating on a small place. One eighth grader wrote:

> . . . *throughout our visits I realized that having a specific area allows you to notice little things. I felt as if each time I went to my sit area I was turning the knob on a microscope. The details just started popping out and I noticed things that you would never notice in just a glance. (Lexi)*

What a great testimonial to the power of outdoor experience!

Post It—Show It

Set aside a bulletin board and table as your classroom nature center. Try to display items that show what your class has done outdoors as shown in Figure 3.4. Digital pictures of critters or plants found outside, maps of the area, or student work directly related to the outing make clear statements that the outdoor experience is directly related to the indoor classroom.

The display needn't be pretty or glitzy. This isn't for show. You just want to reserve a place where some memories and artifacts of your outdoor treks can be enjoyed and revisited by your students. Keep a variety of field guides nearby so kids can see examples of traditional picture guides as well as dichotomous keys.

Figure 3.4 A designated display table provides a place for closer examination of objects found on the school grounds.

Bring the Outdoors into the Classroom

Bird Feeders

I have a vivid image of Linda Lang's former classroom. She used to teach in one of those wonderful old rooms with creaky wooden floors and lots of wall space. There wasn't much wall to be seen, though, since nearly every square inch was covered—mostly with nature-related posters and student work that reflected the outdoors.

The outside wall was blessed with many windows, one of which had a large pine tree growing nearby. She had placed bird feeders near the windows and the pine provided cover for the birds. Kids busily observed the various species of birds at the feeders and then recorded what they saw. Her class participated in the Classroom FeederWatch program through Cornell University, which actually turns the bird feeder outside the window into an interdisciplinary research activity and enables children to share their data with students across the country. The data is then accessible online and can be compared with findings in other regions. More information about this program is in the "Resources" section at the end of this book.

Placed near classroom windows, feeders can provide a unique opportunity for students to get an up-close look at wildlife without leaving the classroom (see Figure 3.5). Feeders also can promote a stewardship ethic as students take responsibility for filling and maintaining the feeders.

Figure 3.5 A bank of several bird feeders provides almost continuous opportunities to watch wildlife.

Feeders also provide a great opportunity to carry the message of enjoying nature back to the home. Simple bird feeders can be made from a variety of simple materials and often require no construction. Pie pans, plastic bottles, and pine cones with peanut butter and seeds can be converted easily into bird feeders that kids can watch at home. Linda feels that this carryover factor is one of the most important outcomes of outdoor-based teaching. If kids get excited about something they see in nature, hopefully they will develop and share a sense of caring and concern for the environment.

Classroom Pets

Having some plants or domestic animals in the classroom can provide a strong personal link with nature. Even things as simple as a small aquarium or some indoor plants on the windowsill can provide a natural feel to the classroom. If students take on the tasks of cleaning, feeding, watering, and generally taking care of these living things, feelings of responsibility and stewardship begin to develop.

Some teachers have found classroom pets to be valuable teaching tools. I've seen classrooms with gerbils, hamsters, mice, rats, snakes, even ants and worm farms! The decision whether or not to keep a live animal in a classroom is one that needs to be considered carefully, however. Multiple factors need to be evaluated, such as:

- amount of care needed
- purchase or donation of the animal
- health needs of the animal
- cages or other environment
- weekend and vacation arrangements
- cost of feeding and maintaining the animal
- student allergies or other health concerns
- appropriateness of the animal for your classroom

The pet should be included in the classroom only if it can be justified as a way to teach learning objectives throughout the year. The modeling of humane and compassionate animal care is essential. Several outstanding websites are referenced in this book's "Resources" section that provide a useful background for making a decision concerning pets in the classroom.

"When Do We Go Out Again?"

Ask students how frequently they would like to go outside for instruction and the response most likely would be, "every day!" Going outside frequently, and often on the spur of the moment, can certainly invigorate a classroom. But outdoor teaching needs to be planned carefully so that it retains the impact that comes from a change of pace and place.

Outdoor teaching is appealing and engaging, but, like any other teaching method, it can lose its effectiveness if overused. As L. B. Sharp, an early pioneer in experiential education, noted decades ago:

That which can best be learned inside the classroom should be learned there.
That which can best be learned in the out-of-doors through direct experience,
dealing with native materials and life situations, should there be learned.
(1943, 363)

That's good advice. There are many concepts and learning objectives that, frankly, are better taught within a classroom setting where special resources and electronic media are readily available. We need to take a careful look at the curriculum and see where outdoor instruction fits best or could enhance the indoor component of instruction. Good outdoor instruction isn't meant to replace indoor learning; rather, the goal is to enhance and supplement what is being taught within the classroom walls.

Chapter 4

Developing Process Skills in an Engaging Environment

It was an odd sight—twenty students wearing blindfolds and sitting in a circle on the grass. They were holding small sticks about 8 inches long and were slowly turning the sticks over and over in their hands. Little fingers gently touched every inch of bark, frequently stopping to go back again to a tiny raised blemish or branching point of the twig.

This usually animated group of fourth graders was totally focused. The task was to know your twig so well that you could immediately find it again when the sticks were placed in a pile and the blindfolds removed. Amazingly every twig was successfully reunited with its owner! Using only their sense of touch, kids were able to notice very subtle differences. The teacher was pleased—his students had practiced observation from a fresh perspective.

Thus far, we have explored the benefits of outdoor learning for both students and teachers and have described some ways to make the schoolyard a useful outdoor teaching site. We also focused on some of the questions and concerns that arise as teachers consider using the outdoors for instruction—the "nuts and bolts" that can make or break schoolyard-enhanced learning. I hope this information has encouraged you to give schoolyard-enhanced learning a try.

Now let's take a look at some specific examples of activities that work especially well outside. The activities are presented in two chapters. This chapter focuses on using the outdoors to teach process skills, and the next addresses specific content areas.

Process-Skills Activities

Although it would be ideal if you have some of the school site enhancements outlined in Chapter 2, most of the activities described in this chapter require nothing more than a grassy area. As one of our eighth-grade philosophers, Conor, said, "You can find a lot of things if you just keep a sharp eye and pay attention to the ground in front of you."

Process skills can be taught either indoors or out. However, by occasionally going outside to focus on cross-disciplinary skills such as observing and describing, we can add welcome variety to instruction. Another less obvious benefit, though, is that frequent experiences in nature can help kids to feel comfortable in the outdoors—and that just might be the most valuable outcome of all for today's techno-saturated generation.

Every content area has its own unique set of knowledge, skills, and values, but there are certain process skills that cut across content lines and are important in most all fields of study. For example, being able to analyze data, information, or situations is just as important in social studies as it is in science, mathematics, or literature. Likewise, observing, describing, classifying, organizing, inferring, predicting, and evaluating have universal application.

When we cover certain topics as teachers, we want to emphasize one or more of these process skills. By going outdoors and using the activities listed here, a skill can be practiced in a context that is unusual yet engaging. For example, if the upcoming topic is descriptive writing in language arts, it's both appropriate and motivating to take students outside to sharpen their observational skills in nature and then go indoors for a writing task.

Over the years, I have had wonderful opportunities to try out a variety of outdoor activities with many schools and different grade levels. Children very quickly help you separate the really effective ideas from the ones that look good on paper put don't work well outside. The examples in this section are the clear-cut winners! These are the ones that I use repeatedly because they are the most highly engaging and also can be adapted to a wide grade range. Teachers have also consistently confirmed that these are the outdoor activities that they use most often to teach general process skills.

Skill Quest: Tale of the Tape
Process skill(s): observing/describing
Time needed: 20–30 minutes
Suggested grade range: 4–8

In a nutshell: *Leaves and long paper strips are used to focus on observation and description.*
What you will need: *Masking tape, leaves or other natural objects, roll of adding machine tape*

The Details

The success of this activity comes in part from the unique writing surface—a 3-foot long piece of adding machine tape. Each student is given a strip of the paper, a leaf (all of which come from the same bush or tree), and a piece of masking tape. Students tape the leaf to the top of the strip and write as many words or phrases as possible that describe something about the leaf (see Figure 4.1). Encourage them to fill the tape with descriptive words! Allow enough time for the "furrowed brow" to develop. The first ten or twelve items are usually pretty easy to do—it's the next ten or fifteen that really force close observation and creative thinking. Let students remove the leaf from the paper to get a better look.

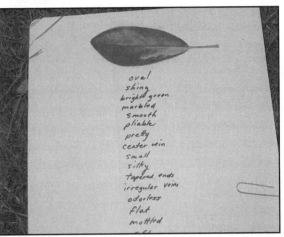

Figure 4.1 Students use a 2- or 3-foot strip of adding machine tape to record a long list of words or phrases that describe the leaf at the top. This unusual writing surface works well to foster creative thinking.

83

When you see that most have exhausted their word banks, ask a volunteer to read his or her list very slowly. As the list is read, students should check off items that are the same or very similar to what they have written. You can also have one student keep a master list of all the words that are generated. As others read the items that they still have unmarked, continue to add to the master list.

Although I have used this activity successfully both inside and outside, it has maximum impact when done outside. There is something about nature that seems to pull at all the senses and heighten creativity.

Making the Most of It

Depending on your objective and the age of the students, your follow-up discussion can take a variety of turns. You can simply emphasize that there are many words that can be used to describe a simple object. For a class of twenty, you will probably come up with more than one hundred different descriptive words. It's a valuable learning experience for kids just to see that people can look at the same object and see many different things. That in itself is a springboard into a social studies lesson!

It's also interesting to have students look at their lists and see if they can find any patterns. Often, you can quickly tell who has the scientific bent in the group (lobed, chlorophyll, food factory), or the artistic (emerald green, symmetrical) or the tactile (rough, soft, fuzzy). Kids quickly see that the mind gets in one track for awhile and generates descriptors all of one type. When that well goes dry, the brain dips into another source.

Extending and Adapting

This activity is a great way to emphasize the power of careful observation—a critical skill in any content area. Teachers use this activity very successfully as a motivator or introduction to the study of adjectives and descriptive writing. It's a good one to use prior to any activity that demands rich description or careful observation.

Not much adaptation is needed for varying grade levels. Of course, higher grade levels will generate more complex and varied descriptive words or phrases. At upper grade levels, the activity can serve as an entry into a topic (e.g., use stones instead of leaves as an introduction to a geology unit). I know some high school science teachers who use it prior to a study of plants.

Teachers have used many items for this activity. Stones, twigs, leaves, and even kernels of corn have been taped to the paper strips. It's most effective to use natural materials that come from the same source (like twigs from the same tree, or corn kernels from the same ear). The power of this activity emerges when students realize that a wide diversity of observations can be generated from looking at very similar objects.

Skill Quest: Find Something That . . .

Process skill(s): observing
Time needed: about 20–30 minutes
Suggested grade range: K–8 (these can be adapted to any grade or level of sophistication)

In a nutshell: This section could be subtitled "scavenger hunts." The basic idea is simple—give students instructions to locate specific types of items in nature.

The Details

Careful observation is a critical skill that, unfortunately, is being eroded in our culture by electronic media manipulating our attention. The activities described here focus attention on specific aspects of the schoolyard environment and, hopefully, help students to become more attuned to the richness of their surroundings. Here are some examples of focused scavenger hunts.

What's Out of Place?

Objects are placed in a natural setting and students look carefully to see what is out of place. The ideal location is a hedgerow or overgrown area that borders a mowed area. Over a span of 30 to 50 feet, place both unnatural objects as well as natural items that are simply out of place (e.g., broccoli or onions wouldn't be found in a tree). Any manufactured article works well also—pencils, rubber bands, lightbulbs, scouring pads, mustard, CDs, sponges, artificial flowers—you get the idea. Just clean out your junk drawer at home!

Tuck the objects amongst the natural foliage being careful to vary the height where you place the objects. I have found that it works best to have kids walk in pairs to locate the objects and keep a count. At the end, debrief what was found and then have kids walk back the opposite way to see if they can find additional items.

This is probably my favorite outdoor awareness activity. Although it sounds very simple, it is incredibly engaging. Kids of all ages quickly get caught up in the hunt and focus intently. It also is an activity where the class scholar is frequently not the one who sees the most.

One Midwest high school biology teacher took this activity to a new level by carefully hiding pots of nonnative houseplants in the ground cover. Although the cactus was a giveaway, some of the other ornamental species tucked among the native foliage along the path really looked like they belonged there. You can make the activity even more challenging by including rocks that are not found in your area, or even creating animal tracks from nonlocal species. (Based on the activity "Unnature Trail," from Cornell 1979)

Shapes and Patterns

Shapes or patterns can be drawn individually on index cards or several of them can be placed on a sheet. Students look for examples of the shapes or patterns in nature. This activity has both a micro and a macro dimension, as can be seen in Figures 4.2a and 4.2b. For example, have students look for parallel lines in small items like leaves or twigs; then have them look up and find the same concept in a macro version such as two trees standing side by side. A wavy line can be seen in a crooked twig as well as in the distant hills.

Figures 4.2a and 4.2b A micro version of parallel lines can be found outdoors in leaf venation. You can also ask students to look for parallel lines by taking a macro view of an area. There are at least a dozen examples of parallel lines in this playground scene.

Although this is a very simple activity, it focuses attention and results in some very creative observations. I prefer to use index cards that can be shuffled and redistributed as kids find examples. Shape cards have been a boon during hikes. When the group starts to get a little antsy, I pull out the cards and give one to each student. As we walk along, I periodically hand a new card to the person behind me who then gives his card to the next person, giving everyone a chance to get a new card. It helps to do a few practice shapes as a whole group so that everyone gets the macro-micro concept.

Instead of using shape and pattern cards, middle grades teacher Laura Grimm has creatively morphed this idea into a shapes and patterns bingo card (see Figure 4.3). She simply took the various shapes and put them on a bingo grid, making several versions of the card so everyone doesn't get bingo at the same time. The sheets are laminated and the kids use crayon to mark the items as they are found. The plastic keeps the sheets dry and reusable, and the crayon can be wiped off at the end of the activity.

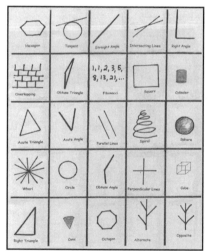

Figure 4.3 If the shape card has been laminated, students can mark off items that they find with a crayon. The marks can be easily wiped off and the cards are ready to be used again. The goal is to find items in nature that resemble the shape. The various shapes can also be placed individually on index cards and "dealt" to students as they explore a natural area.

Color Match

This is great observation activity especially at the K–4 grade range. I use paint chip samples that are available from home improvement stores. You don't need many and most stores are very willing to help out a teacher.

I really like the paint samples that have four or five variations of the same color on one strip. Kids can go out and try to match up a natural item with the color on the chip. A variation is to take a piece of masking tape and place it sticky side up along one side of the colors. Kids then take little samples of the color they find (fingernail size) and place them on the tape. For preschool- or kindergarten-age youngsters, it can work well to give out an index card or paint sample with just one color.

Themed Scavenger Hunts

These are limited only by your creativity! The format can be either index cards with individual items or a list that is used as a check sheet to find items. Both work well. The index card approach is effective if you want to keep a group around you. The list, of course, sends kids off in a variety of directions.

Here are a few ideas for themed scavenger hunts that may spark the imagination.

Sensory
Find a soft object, something that makes a sound, something that smells good, something sticky, something prickly.

Content Related
Find items related to a book that students just read.
Alphabet scavenger hunt: Gather an item for each letter of the alphabet.
Fibonacci hunt: Find items in nature that illustrate 1, 2, 3, 5, 8, 13, 21 . . .
Geometry hunt: Find rectangles in nature (or circles, squares, triangles, and so on).
Trees: Find a leaf, a snag, a rotting log, a pine cone . . .
Animal homes: Look for bird's nest, squirrel nest, insect home . . . (Be sure to stress that homes not be disturbed!)
Find ten examples of weathering.
Find ten examples of camouflage.

Creative Hunts
Whimsical: Find something funny, something sad, something old, something young.
Disappearing items: Find things that will not be here next year, next month, tomorrow.

Hunts That Answer Questions
"What could be used to build houses?"
"What is food for a squirrel?"
"What has hundreds of animals living in it?"

Themed scavenger hunts allow for many possible answers and can be excellent motivators as new concepts are being introduced. They can be easily tailored to complement specific units or topics that you are studying.

A Techno Twist

Digital cameras can add a unique variation to the traditional scavenger hunt. Students still look for specific items, but they take pictures of them once they

Safety and Stewardship

Use the outdoor experience to also emphasize good stewardship. A scavenger hunt can send the wrong message if kids scatter across the landscape randomly pulling up plants or disturbing animal homes and habitats in a mad rush to check every item off the list. Most problems occur when the scavenger hunt is turned into a race ("Let's see who can find everything first!"). Stress that students should avoid removing natural materials (show it rather than pick it), replace anything that is examined, and return rocks and logs to their original placement

With any scavenger hunt, it is essential to emphasize basic safety considerations such as cautions about poison ivy or other dangerous plants, reminders about hazards that may exist on the site, and the need for clear boundaries. Make boundaries very obvious by using flags or clothesline to define an area. In a wooded area, consider placing strips of masking tape on the trunks of trees to define your boundary area.

are located. It's a great way to let everyone see what was found without disturbing the natural setting.

If you have access to GPS devices, you can even have students mark the items found as waypoints and then download the points onto a map of the site. There is relatively inexpensive software available that will automatically link a photo to a GPS waypoint and allow you to click on a map location and see the picture of an item at that spot. Try taking the scavenger hunt to the digital level!

Skill Quest: They Belong Together
Process skill(s): *classifying/organizing*
Time needed: *45–60 minutes*
Suggested grade range: *4–8*

In a nutshell: *Students collect natural items and then sort them into determined categories.*
What you will need: *paper plates, index cards*

The Details

Working in groups of two or three, students gather at least fifteen different, small, natural items (living or nonliving) for their group. The objects can be very simple such as a stone, twig, leaf, blades of grass, and so on. Once the items are collected, give each group three paper plates and ask them to come up with three categories that can be used to divide all of the items. They write the categories represented by each plate on the index cards and place them under the appropriate plates.

Have groups circulate and look at each others' plates and try to guess what system was used. They then can lift the plate and read the categories.

One teacher has extra index cards by each plate and lets each group write down its guess of the categories that were used. It's a real "aha" experience for the original group to see how others interpret the groupings on the plates.

Making the Most of It

It works best to tell students that they can't use vague categories such as: big, medium, small; or dark, medium, light. You want them to stretch a bit to find similarities and differences.

Skill Quest: Shades of Green
Process skill(s): organizing/discriminating detail
Time needed: 30–45 minutes
Suggested grade range: 2–8

In a nutshell: Students collect small samples of a color in nature and then place them in order from lightest to darkest.

What you will need: strips of cardboard or oak tag approximately 3 inches wide and 18–24 inches long, masking tape

The Details

As they sit outside, ask students how many shades of green they see. The usual response is anywhere from three to five. Working in pairs, students collect small samples (about thumbnail size) of differing shades of green they find in the schoolyard. Usually, I ask pairs to bring in twelve to fifteen samples. As the groups return, give each a cardboard strip that has a piece of masking tape fastened sticky side up along the entire length. The group's task then is to look carefully at the samples collected and arrange them from lightest to darkest on the cardboard strip. After the strips are completed, I have students lay them on the ground and we have a color gallery for all to see.

Things just don't get any greener than in the spring. I took a sixth-grade class outside on one of those perfect spring days, paired up the kids and explained "shades of green." The goal was to find at least twelve different shades of green. Without really thinking, I added that a group last year had found twenty items. One pair of boys quickly came back with their dozen tiny samples and boasted that they could find at least ten more different shades (breaking last year's "record"). Another pair overheard the conversation and said that they also could find more than twenty examples.

The end result was that we had two pairs that needed three cardboard strips to display their findings! Of course, a person from a group that stuck with the original task smugly pointed out that several of the samples really looked the same. That probably was true—I'm sure that upon careful examination there most certainly were duplicates. On the other hand, so what! The eager beavers had a great time exploring the outdoors with an intensity that they probably had never experienced before.

Now, I'm not advocating that you turn "shades of green" into a competition. It just so happened that this class had some kids who really enjoyed creating their own challenges. This experience reinforced for me the energy and enthusiasm that can build in an outdoor setting. Kids who normally turned to video games for excitement were getting a kick out of looking at leaves and stems!

89

Making the Most of It

This activity vividly demonstrates the huge diversity of color in nature. Students quickly see that even one leaf may have many different shades, and usually has a completely different shade on the top than on the bottom. In fact, parts of one leaf  can end up in two or three places on the cardboard strip. I like this activity for two reasons. It challenges students to discriminate among many shades of the same color and it also gets kids outside taking a very careful micro look at their surroundings.

The activity is wonderful for developing an attention to detail and works especially well if you limit the "search area" to a rather small space. Be sure to explain the National Wildlife Federation's "1-in-20" rule mentioned in Chapter 3 and emphasize that only a sample the size of a thumbnail is needed.

This is an activity that guarantees success. Everyone ends up with color strips that look pretty cool! One example is shown in Figure 4.4.

Figure 4.4 Students easily find many examples of differing shades of green on the school grounds. They then arrange the small samples from darkest to lightest on a piece of cardboard with masking tape placed sticky side up.

90

Extending and Adapting

Although green is a very easy color to find in most seasons of the year, other colors work just as well. In the fall, shades of red or orange are effective. I have even done this activity in winter as shades of grey, using bits of fallen twigs, dead leaves, dried grasses, and so on. (Based on the activity "Color Chains," Van Matre 1974)

Skill Quest: Nature Analogies

Process skill(s): analyze, infer, synthesize, comprehend
Time needed: 20–30 minutes
Suggested grade range: 4–8

In a nutshell: This activity really hits many of Bloom's higher-order thinking skills. Students explain how common household objects are similar in form or function to items in nature.

What you will Need: Empty your kitchen junk drawer and unload the workbench! Most any small, nonnatural household item will work: cotton balls, rubber gloves, tweezers, eraser, rubber band, paper clip, lightbulb, old CD, nails, old cell phone, roll of masking tape, cup, bandage, fork, spoon, paintbrush, marker.

The Details

This activity works well with students in groups of two or three. Place your collected items in a bag and have kids pull out an item for each group. The challenge is for the pair or threesome to come up with a way that the item is similar to a plant, animal, or natural feature.

The similarity can relate to the form or shape, or to some function. For example, the rubber glove is like the protective covering provided by the bark of a tree (function); cotton balls are like puffy clouds (form). Have each small group share its analogies with the entire class. Have other groups add their ideas also. You can then either put all the items back in the bag and draw again, or, if you have enough items left, have pairs draw from the remaining items. This is another activity that could be done indoors but has much more impact and relevance if done outside.

Making the Most of It

I am always amazed at the creativity that this simple activity generates. One fourth grader said that a CD was like the growth rings of a tree since they both could tell a story!

A lot is going on mentally here—kids have to draw on their prior knowledge of plant and animal characteristics and then use inference and synthesis to come up with an analogy. This activity is effective whenever higher order thinking skills are being emphasized or when a change of pace is desired (adapted from Stokes 1986).

Skill Quest: Tree Texture

Process skill(s): observation, analysis, inference, visual discrimination
Time needed: 30 minutes
Suggested grade range: 3–6

In a nutshell: Students locate a tree by using only a bark rubbing of the trunk.
What you will need: paper (legal size), crayons, masking tape

The Details

You need a location that has as many trees as you have students. The trees should be in the same general area so that you can easily monitor the activity. Place a strip of masking tape on the bark of the trees you want to use. Each child takes a piece of paper and a crayon (with the paper removed), and heads for a tree marked with tape. The paper should be placed at about chin height and a bark rubbing should be made on the same side as the tape. After completion, ask students to turn the paper over and write a secret password (e.g., name of a pet or mother's first name). It's important that kids don't just put their own names on the back since they will tend to remember where each person had been, making the task too easy.

91

When everyone is finished, shuffle the papers well and give one to every chil[d]. The task is to look at the rubbing and then try to guess which tree it came from. Whe[n] students think they have found a match, they should look on the back and call out th[e] identifier to find out if they were correct. As each tree is correctly identified, the tap[e] should be removed—this makes the task a little easier for those who are still looking. If you have a small group, or to make the task more challenging, mark more trees o[r] items than there are students.

Making the Most of It

One third-grade teacher liked the concept of exploring textures outdoors, bu[t] just did not have enough trees conveniently located on the school grounds. Instea[d] of exploring just tree bark texture, she expanded the activity to include all types o[f] surfaces. She placed tape on a variety of items, including brick, pavement, boulder[s], wood, metal, glass, and playground equipment. She asked students to do th[e] rubbings near the location of the tape (a hands-length away) to make it easier to d[o] the matchups. The variety of textures was amazing and kids were asking to do extr[a] rubbings just to see what they might find.

Another variation of this activity is to take a sheet of paper and fold it into fourth[s] or eighths. Students then take their crayons and do rubbings of objects they find i[n] the vicinity, one rubbing in each square. They can either label the squares and shar[e] their product with the group, or the unlabeled sheets can be exchanged and kids ca[n] try to locate the objects.

Skill Quest: Nanohike
Process skill(s): observation, description, analysis, evaluation
Time needed: 60 minutes
Suggested grade range: 3–6

In a nutshell: Students design mini "trails" using a few yards of yarn.
What you will need: 3–4 yards of yarn or string

The Details

This is an activity that works best in pairs. Give each group a length of yarn an[d] ask each to look carefully at the surrounding area. The objective is to lay out a "trail" with the yarn that will include a number of points of natural interest that are marked with sticks. For example, students might include an interesting plant, spiderweb, moss, unusual stone or rock, nibbled leaf, animal home, and such. You can set the number of expected points of interest based upon the age of the students. I usually like to have at least eight points marked if 4 yards of yarn are used.

After the trails are laid out, tell students that they are now rangers in the world's smallest national park. Have students take each other for a nanohike on their trails, explaining why the various points were included.

Making the Most of It

This activity can work well in the schoolyard, especially where mowed areas meet the unmowed. The more mowed and manicured the area, the longer you may want to make the yarn!

You need to be clear with students that you want them to point out interesting natural features. It's effective to make a sample trail and explain a few points of interest to model what you want students to do. I have found that if you don't clearly emphasize that you want them to describe real, natural things, younger kids especially will create exaggerated points of interest that are creative but may miss the real-world description that you want (a small hole becomes a " giant's cave"). On the other hand, maybe it is just as effective to vary this activity and do it as a fantasy nanohike!

The general idea for this activity has been around for a long time. I first saw it in print as "micro trails" in the book Acclimatizing by Steve Van Matre, in which there is a beautiful example of a "tour" that a student might give of a micro trail:

> Here we have a little purple thing that you wouldn't usually see if you were just walking along. Take a look at the lacework on the underside of this leaf—isn't it amazing? Here is a colony of moss—a whole community growing right here! This is what we call a silver trumpet. It's only about a fourth of an inch tall, but we see how neat it looks through this lens. Here is the entrance to an underground spider's nest. Look inside and see if you can find him. Down here we have something of Mother Nature; this used to be a stick, but now it's becoming fertilizer. This plant has a disease. And here we have another helper of Mother Nature: this used to be a trunk, but now it's a place for all of the little things to grow. A dragonfly helped me out here—he left his wing; it's really delicate. And last, we come to the lichen lands. They almost look like coral, don't they? (1974, 81)

More than three decades later, the activity still has an obvious impact on this Ohio eighth grader:

> What I liked most was the activity where we were able to create a little park with the string. I love being creative, and I had to be with the little string that I had . . . it taught me that there is more to this big world than you realize. You can find a lot of things if you just keep a sharp eye and pay attention to the ground in front of you.
>
> —Conor

93

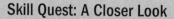

Skill Quest: A Closer Look

Process skill(s): observation, description, comparison
Time needed: 15–20 minutes
Suggested grade range: 1–8

In a nutshell: Students retrieve their stones from a pile of similar ones.

What you will need: As many small stones or pebbles as there are students, plus a few more stones to add to the challenge

The Details

Each student takes a stone from the container. The directions are:

· *Take a very careful look at your stone.*
· *Turn it over; look for different colors.*
· *Feel the rough and smooth parts of your stone.*
· *Does its shape remind you of something?*
· *Turn it over again in your hand to look at it even more closely.*
· *Put the stone down in front of you. Rub your hands together rapidly; now clap the top of each hand; now clap your hands together loudly and vigorously. (I include the hand-clapping directions to focus attention on the tactile dimension of the stone, and, frankly, also to add a gimmick that keeps kids engaged.)*
· *Pick up your stone again, and pass it gently over the palm of your hand, now over the top of your hand, now across your cheek.*
· *Next place all of the stones back in the container.*

You then mix all of the stones in the container and pour them out on the ground. Students then try to find their own stones once again. Have students tell how they were able to locate their stones.

Key Point to Emphasize

Say to your students that most people would say what they did was impossible—all gravel looks basically the same. But they took the time to look at something very closely, and were able to see details that would have been easily missed.

Making the Most of It

This is a very adaptable activity that illustrates two big ideas:

· *Careful observation can reveal many details.*
· *Things that look very similar at a quick glance may really be unique.*

Those concepts can be applied to a multitude of learnings. For example, this activity is frequently used in a guidance context to make the point that all of us, like the stones, are unique and have very distinguishing characteristics. In fact, I first saw this activity used in a children's sermon!

The beauty of this activity is that it can be adapted for most any age level. The older the student, the more alike the stones should be. For young children, you can use stones of obviously different color and shape. For older kids, you can use gravel that is much the same size and color, and you can include 50 percent more stones than students. This activity can also be modified using leaves or twigs. For the ultimate challenge, try using kernels of corn or pumpkin seeds!

Skill Quest: Plant Close-Up

Process skill(s): observation, description
Time needed: 45 minutes
Suggested grade range: 4–8

In a nutshell: Students examine all of the major parts of a plant.
What you will need: Self-Directed Plant Awareness Study Guide from Appendix A

The Details

This activity works just fine on the school lawn. It is effective when done either independently or in pairs. Help students choose a small plant to examine. Dandelions, crab grass, clover, or any type of lawn weed or plant is fine to use. This is a good time to remind about poison ivy or other plants to avoid in your area.

Unless you have a manicured school lawn, I have found that the schoolyard provides an abundance of common plants that can be examined. Emphasize the fact that there should be many more of the same plant nearby if the roots are going to be examined. Have kids spread out so that your sampling won't have too much impact on the lawn.

Students just work their way through the questions on the Self-Directed Plant Awareness Study Guide sheet. Although it may not be possible to do all of the items on the sheet, there can still be a rich observational experience.

Making the Most of It

This activity provides a wonderful opportunity for kids to look very closely at plants they walk by (and over!) every day. The Study Guide in Appendix A does a wonderful job of focusing attention on the parts of a plant in a systematic way and *places heavy emphasis upon sensory awareness. Unfortunately, I do not know th source of the Study Guide Sheet—it has been around a long time!*

Skill Quest: Resource Auction
Process skill(s): comparison, analysis, evaluation
Time needed: 60 minutes
Suggested grade range: 5–8

In a nutshell: Students decide what makes for a good community.
What you will need: The activity centers around the items that follow. Create colorfu signs (8 × 14 is good) that depict each item. You also will need a bidding sheet (see Appendix B) and play money. In using this activity with sixth graders, I usually give each "community" 100,000 dollars in play money.

wide-screen plasma TV for each home	many beautiful shade trees
minivan for every family	large community pool
twenty-screen movie theater	large park
good library	giant fast-food court
clear lake and streams	playing fields for sports
forest of big, old trees	nature center
hiking and biking paths	large shopping mall
large golf course	new housing development

The Details

Of course, this is not meant to be a realistic auction. It really is an exercise in seeing the difference between wants and needs, as well as evaluating positive and negative effects of choices.

Set the Stage

Divide your class into at least three "communities," but not more than six. The size of the community is not too important, as long as there is an opportunity for everyone to provide input.

Tell the groups that they are town council members who have just received a grant that has to be spent to improve their towns. Their job is to decide what items to buy that will be of most value to the community.

Before the bidding starts, each community needs to decide which items it wants to buy and what the top bid will be, keeping in mind that all of the money should be

96

expended by the end of the auction. This discussion and decision-making process are really the heart of the activity and should not be rushed.

Each community also needs to identify three people:
· spokesperson (bidder)
· treasurer (holds the money and pays for purchased items)
· recorder (carefully logs what was bought and for how much)

Frequently remind the groups of two key points:
1) At the end of the auction, all money should be gone.
2) Communities should buy as many items as possible (saving all of your money for one or two items doesn't make for a balanced community!).

After communities have selected their items and top bids, the auction begins. Just the spokesperson can bid. Allow bids to jump only in 500-dollar increments to build excitement, rather than letting everyone immediately go to their maximums. The bidder can exceed the group's maximum determined bid only if there is agreement by the entire community. As a community wins the bid, the treasurer pays for the item and then receives the picture of what was purchased.

The auction continues until half of the listed items have been sold. At the halfway point, tell the communities that they can have another town meeting and look at how much money they have left and what is left on their lists. They now can change their choices and top bids. This is also a very critical part of the activity since most groups now see that they have not been able to get several of the items that they wanted. They need to reevaluate what is left in terms of benefit to their towns. Some of the most valuable discussions take place at this point in the activity.

The bidding continues until all items have been "sold." At the end, each group shows what they have purchased, tells how much cash is left, and explains how the decisions were made.

Making the Most of It

This activity generates a tremendous amount of good discussion. It forces everyone to evaluate a wide array of options and is an excellent segue into a discussion of the environmental impact of our actions.

This is an adaptation of an activity developed as a rainy-day option by a resident outdoor education program many years ago. Although the original intent was to use the activity indoors, the excitement created by the auction environment produces a great deal of noise. Since this is a loud activity, it's a perfect one to do outside. An outdoor setting for this activity also seems to stimulate more interest in paying top dollar for some of the nature items in the mix!

Hopefully this chapter encourages you to think about using the outdoors to develop process skills. Teaching with an outdoor twist may provide the enthusiasm and engagement that help students see skills such as observing, describing, classifying, organizing, predicting, and evaluating in new ways.

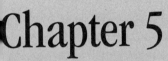

Chapter 5

Teaching Content-Area Concepts Outdoors

The outdoors can facilitate learning in two ways:

1) The schoolyard can provide a venue, or backdrop, for an activity (e.g., going outside to read a story).

2) The schoolyard can provide the content and serve as an essential element of an activity (e.g., going outside to use a statistical sampling technique to estimate the population of ants in the school lawn).

Both approaches are very valid uses of schoolyard-enhanced learning. In both cases the outdoors serves as an instructional resource and provides a valuable change of pace and place. Just the simple act of occasionally going outside for class and using the schoolyard as a classroom can energize a lesson and refocus attention.

This section is organized by traditional content areas. The goal is to provide a few ideas for using the schoolyard to teach material related to content standards or objectives. The activities presented here are meant as "pump primers"—ideas that, hopefully, will spark your imagination and creativity as you consider the components of your curriculum that could be enhanced on the schoolyard.

Although I have tried to identify some major concepts that could be effectively taught through an outdoor setting, I'm sure that a content specialist could find many other ways to incorporate the schoolyard. The "Resources" section at the end of this book also includes references to a variety of materials that provide content-specific outdoor activities.

The examples in this chapter are meant only to reinforce and enhance, not replace, indoor classroom instruction. Effective teaching requires varied approaches, both indoors and out. By occasionally using outdoor instruction to enhance what is being done inside, we can create a varied learning environment. The outdoors can be the critical experiential link that transforms an abstract concept into a concrete learning experience.

Mathematics

Mathematics has many topics that can be complemented through outdoor activities. When the schoolyard provides real-world examples, abstract mathematical concepts become more understandable.

In 2000, the National Council of Teachers of Mathematics (NCTM) published *Principles and Standards for School Mathematics,* which has become a major resource for state and local curriculum development. There are three general areas of the mathematics standards that I feel are especially appropriate for schoolyard-enhanced learning:

1) measurement
2) geometry
3) data analysis and probability

Of course, these three topics can overlap. For example, measurement is often involved in geometry as concepts such as area and volume are explored. Measurement of objects or distances outdoors can also generate data for comparison and analysis. Here are some activities that teachers have suggested to reinforce concepts that are being taught in the three areas.

Laura Grimm has two doors in her fifth-grade classroom. Very conveniently, one of them opens directly to the schoolyard! Although this creative teacher uses the outdoors as both venue and content for nearly all areas of the curriculum, her use of the outdoors for mathematics is especially interesting. She incorporates measurement, geometry, and data generation concepts into an outdoor setting. Here are a few examples of how she teaches math concepts using the schoolyard.

Angles

Using popsicle sticks and a string (20–24 feet), students form various shapes, angles, parallel lines, perpendicular lines, and such on the lawn. By shifting the concept from a drawing on paper to a more tangible feature outdoors, the concept is reinforced and can be quickly checked for understanding. This activity can easily be extended by having students take pictures of various types of angles that they find in nature.

Data Generation

Part of Laura's math curriculum involves charting, graphing, and simple statistics. Although textbooks provide data to use in examples, Laura finds it much more effective to occasionally use the outdoors to generate real data for students to use.

Charting Information

101

Water evaporation is a great example of an activity that has science connections and also serves as a data generator. On a sunny day, Laura takes a cup of water and pours it on a level area of sidewalk or asphalt. She uses chalk to draw a line around the shape that was formed by the pool of water. After waiting ten to fifteen minutes, she draws another line around the new shape. The procedure continues until all of the water is gone. Next, students take string and lay it on top of the outer shape. They then measure the length of string needed to outline the perimeter. Students continue to calculate the perimeter of all of the shapes that were drawn and then chart the data.

In the human bar graph activity, the outdoors can be very effective as a venue. For this activity, group students according to birth month and then go outside to the blacktop play area. They lie down at the appropriate month and form a human bar graph, as can be seen in Figure 5.1. The activity is a great icebreaker at the beginning of a school year, and also provides a very real representation of data.

Figure 5.1 This human bar graph visually verifies that most students in this class were born in August.

As an extension activity, Laura has kids line up according to birthdates. The long line is closed to form a circle on the blacktop.

Figures 5.2a and 5.2b Students first form a circle based upon the month in which they were born. The teacher then uses chalk to divide the circle into the various seasons. When students step back there is a visual representation of the distribution of birthdates throughout the four seasons.

Laura then draws lines on the ground to show where the four seasons would fall and an instant circle graph/pie chart is created (see Figures 5.2a and b).

Random Sampling

Students generate data outside that can be later analyzed or utilized indoors. Laura has pairs of students launch rubber bands with yarn attached. The rubber band is placed on the thumb and the student pulls back on the yarn.

What happens next is determined by the type of data that she wants students to gather. A boundary is designated over the area where the rubber band lands (e.g., coat hangers bent into an oval or circle, large round rubber seals or gaskets, loops of string, or even hula hoops). A standardized unit such as a square meter length of cord makes it easy to translate findings into approximations for a much larger area.

Often kids get down on their hands and knees to count and record the number of different plants and animals that they find in the sample area (hand lenses come in handy here). Sometimes the tally may be of specific plant types that are in the sample or the soil type that is present. After recording the information, another launch is made and the process can be quickly repeated.

By going to different areas of the schoolyard, comparisons can be made and inferences and predictions generated. If you know the size of your sample, it is also possible to estimate how many of a certain species there might be in an acre. This activity provides realistic opportunities for statistical analysis and gives students insight into how scientists estimate populations of species in large areas.

I have used a variation of this activity using balloons— the 9 inch round size seems to work well. The basic procedure is to blow up

102

the balloon (don't tie the end), hold it over your head, and let it go. It zooms wildly and then lands; place the ring or boundary over the area where the balloon lands; then begin recording data. A Balloon Launch Data Sheet is available in Appendix C. One disadvantage of the balloon launch is that you have to contend with the squeaks and squawks that kids can generate with balloons!

Having kids work with data that they have collected in an area familiar to them is a great motivator. The abstract concept of data representation suddenly becomes much more concrete.

Data Sources

Although it's ideal to use a grassy schoolyard like Laura's for data generation, it's very possible to utilize the outdoors even when there are no plants or critters available. Here are some examples of creative ways that resourceful teachers have used the outdoors as a data source.

Parking Lot Data

Use the parking lot as a learning tool. Have kids count and then visually represent the numbers of various car colors, models, or the different manufacturers represented.

Cold Data

Cossondra George knows snow! She teaches in the Upper Peninsula of Michigan, known for its winters that generate at least 200 inches of snow a year, with snow on the ground continuously from November through at least the beginning of April. She says, "If we didn't 'enjoy' snow, we'd be stuck inside for most of the school year."

Cossondra uses the wintry weather in a variety of data collection activities, such as:

- temperature charting
- snow-depth readings
- snow-depth comparisons in different locations on the school grounds
- snow-melt predictions
- estimation of the amount of water in a given amount of snow
- estimates of the amount of snow in an area
- calculating the amount of storage needed for removed snow

103

Winter becomes a data source and students get a welcome change of pace and place!

Shapes

To reinforce that geometric figures such as triangles, rectangles, and circles aren't found only in textbooks, Laura uses an outdoor scavenger hunt that includes geometric shapes. It's designed as a Bingo game, with several variations of the cards used so that everyone doesn't win at once.

After the initial scavenger hunt, students use cameras to record outdoor examples of spheres, cylinders, cubes, pyramids, and so on. Students bring in their pictures and the class identifies the geometric figures that are represented. The same approach is effective to show symmetry in nature.

Science

". . . the physical environment in and around the school can be used as a living laboratory for the study of natural phenomena. Whether the school is located in a densely populated urban area, a sprawling suburb, a small town, or a rural area, the environment can and should be used as a resource for science study."

—National Science Education Standards (National Research Council 1996)

Cameras as Tools

Cameras can be great outdoor instructional tools:

- Interesting things found outdoors can be recorded to analyze later inside.
- Habitats are not disturbed.
- They allow kids to act on their interest in gadgets and gizmos.

It's now possible to purchase digital cameras for as low as twenty dollars. Of course, these have very low megapixel ratings, but that really isn't a problem for basic classroom use. Even small images load just fine into presentation software such as PowerPoint. Low prices make it feasible to purchase a grade-level set of cameras that can be shared with other teachers. One camera for every two or three students in a class is ample. Be sure that the cameras can download to a computer. Disposable digital cameras are cheaper, but not nearly as flexible an option.

Parent organizations often are looking for projects. As little as 200 dollars could provide a set of inexpensive digital cameras to share with all grade levels. Since there is no film or processing, the usage cost is very low, with the main expense being occasional battery replacement.

This is a powerful endorsement for the use of the schoolyard to enhance science learning. Science is the content area that most people first associate with outdoor instruction. The areas of life science, physical science, and earth and space science all can be enhanced by using the outdoors as an instructional tool.

It's easy to see how the schoolyard can be used as a natural lab for examining the plants and animals that live there. But the outdoors can be more than just a place to find examples of life science concepts. The schoolyard can provide a great venue, or backdrop, for enhancing the teaching of physical science as well as earth and space science topics.

For example, the schoolyard is a great setting for teaching about relative distances in the solar system. After studying diagrams of the solar system and reading about distances between planets, take the class outside and represent the solar system in the schoolyard. The representations become very dramatic as students translate scaled numbers into paces outdoors. Once again, the outdoors has become a huge laboratory in which to reinforce a concept that was first developed inside.

Real-World Effect

Kristin Metz of the Boston Schoolyard Initiative uses the term *real-world effect* to describe the impact of teaching a concept at the micro level indoors followed by an experience outdoors on a macro level.

Kristin tells of a Boston teacher who uses the schoolyard as a venue to enhance a lesson on simple machines. After talking about and demonstrating levers and pulleys indoors, the class moves outside and uses a block and tackle to lift the teacher several feet off the ground. Of course the activity generates a lot of laughs and excitement, but students have moved beyond pictures and miniature models and now can see a macro version of the concept.

Another teacher taught basic principles of magnetism indoors that included testing objects to see what was attracted to a magnet. The teacher then took the class outdoors and had kids check for materials around the school that were attracted to a magnet. Kids later wrote about the experience in their science notebooks and, interestingly, wrote the most about the objects that they found outside.

Students were making small parachutes as a part of a science lesson. Although they first experimented indoors by dropping the parachutes from a chair, the real "aha" experience came when they took the little parachutes outside and tossed them in the air. One child stood transfixed as his parachute was carried by the wind for 30 feet. As Kristin noted, "The outdoor experience can show you something very different that is impossible to duplicate indoors."

The real-world effect certainly makes sense. By replicating a concept outdoors that was experienced on a smaller scale indoors, you are building upon a child's immediate past experience and providing a somewhat different view of the same concept. In addition, you are reinforcing the fact that concepts taught in the classroom also have application beyond the school walls.

Going outside is not something unusual to students in Josh Flory's eighth-grade science classes. He uses the school grounds effectively as both a backdrop for learning as well as for the content of instruction. Here are a few examples from Josh's plan book.

Physical Science

When exploring the properties of air and air pressure, Josh takes his classes outside on a sunny day to inflate a giant solar bag. The bag is made of very thin plastic and is fifty feet long and about two and a half feet in diameter. Kids have to run with the bag to fill it with air. After the bag heats in the sun, it slowly begins to rise, looking like a huge solar tube. Concepts such as solar energy, laws of gases, as well as density and buoyancy take on a more concrete meaning for students when witnessed outdoors.

Earth Science

Josh teaches in a community that has had a lot of construction. Some of the contractors were willing to transport boulders large enough to sit on and he created a small circle on the school grounds. There were many different types of boulders brought in including glacial erratics and some with fossils. The rock circle provides an opportunity to show larger examples of rock types than would be possible in the classroom. It also provides a transition from micro examples indoors to macro exhibits outside. This process of using dual exemplars

Figure 5.3 A boulder circle adds natural interest to an area, and also provides a home base for outdoor instruction.

helps to make abstract concepts much more concrete. It's impressive to see the characteristics of the small stone you examined indoors reflected in a boulder weighing nearly a ton. The rock circle also has the added advantage of serving as an outdoor classroom and seating area, as seen in Figure 5.3.

Life Science

Mr. Flory's eighth-grade students take part in a "sit area" project. Although the focus is life science, there are really three broad objectives that he is trying to accomplish:

1) to develop students' science skills in a natural setting
2) to integrate other content areas (e.g., math, language arts) with science content
3) to nurture an attitude of environmental stewardship

Students select a "sit area" on the school grounds—a small space about 5 meters square. The area has to be within sight of the teacher as he moves around the larger area, and should be at least 10 meters away from another student, to minimize students talking with each other. Once the site has been selected, students mark it with a GPS device. These locations can then be opened in a Google Earth aerial map to show where all of the students have chosen to sit.

The areas are visited approximately once each week in the fall and spring. During the Ohio winter, visits take place twice each month. Each visit has a specific purpose that is discussed in the classroom before going out. Examples of activities might include drawing or sketching a plant in the sit area or recording the number of different bird calls heard at different times of day or in different weather conditions.

The activity is not complex, but it has a profound impact. Students begin to realize that there is life all around them—even in the areas that they routinely rush by as they traverse the school grounds.

One student reflected on her observations as she explored her sit area over a period of many weeks. Early in her reflection she admits that ". . . at the start, [I] was not at all impressed." But as she repeatedly visited her spot she began to see things in a totally different way.

Upon looking closer, I realized that there were tiny things everywhere that proved this patch of land was full of life. Whether it was a teensy flower opening up, or an unknown bird chirping . . . this area was more alive than anything I had ever seen. Nature, I have found, isn't meant to be taken in from the comfort of a chair. You're supposed to get closer . . . live right along with it. (Ellen)

Wow. That's a reflection that gives you goose bumps and leaves no doubt that outdoor learning has an impact! She was definitely sharpening her skills of observation, description, analysis, and evaluation. Although the activity was done as a part of a science unit, she will use these skills in all of her classes.

There is profound meaning in Ellen's frank statement that she was not at all impressed at the start of the activity. An infrequent and content-isolated outdoor experience truly may not be very effective. However, regular use of the outdoors, like with Josh Flory's sit-area project, seems to have a cumulative impact. As outdoor experiences are linked and built upon each other, students begin to see relationships and make observations that are impossible in just a few casual visits or an isolated, one-time visit to a park.

Social Studies

Probably the broadest area of study in the school curriculum has to be the social studies. Dictionary definitions include subjects such as history, government, economics, civics, sociology, geography, and anthropology all under the heading of "social studies."

The concept of place-based education is very useful for teaching many social studies topics. By using the community as a laboratory, abstract concepts can be enhanced and made more real to students. Many educators feel strongly that students must gain an understanding of a concept in terms of their own surroundings first, before being able to see it through a more global lens. When the facilities, institutions, resource persons, and events of a community become a part of the curriculum, complex and abstract concepts can be made authentic and relevant to students. To teach social studies content in isolation from the local community is to waste a very valuable and accessible resource.

Since the focus of this book is the schoolyard, let's take a look at a few ways to teach social studies concepts by taking a class outside the front door. The National Council for the Social Studies includes ten themes as the framework for its curriculum standards. Standard III—people, places, and environments—offers many opportunities for outdoor-enhanced learning. This standard focuses on helping students to answer questions, such as:

Where are things located?

Why are they located where they are?

What patterns are reflected in the groupings of things?
What do we mean by region?
How do landforms change?
What implications do these changes have for people?
(National Council for the Social Studies 1994)
Many of the concepts under this standard are covered in units or classes referred to as geography.

Mapping

Especially in the early grades, the schoolyard can provide a useful site for mapping activities. David Sobel, author of the wonderful book *Mapmaking with Children: Sense of Place Education for the Elementary Years,* notes:

> *Children learn the landscape through walking in it and talking about it. We can extend this naturalistic learning by challenging them to represent their knowing with appropriate media. In the same vein, first mapmaking projects should focus on the narrow scope of the immediate world that the child lives in. The home and school are rich enough environments to serve as the content for children's maps. (1998, 24)*

Map activities can take a variety of formats. Actually, Sobel suggests that a child's first maps should probably be three-dimensional representations or models of an area.

Sobel notes that careful mapping of even a very small area forces us to take a meticulous look at our surroundings. He describes a marine ecology course that he took as a graduate student in which he had to map two tide pools.

> *The more we looked, the more we saw. It wasn't until the fourth day that we discovered whelk egg cases and sea cucumbers. They had been there all along, but we hadn't learned to see them. (1998, 73)*

Those unexpected discoveries and "aha" moments are precisely what outdoor learning can provide for students of all ages, from elementary to graduate school. Sobel suggests having students map sections of the school lawn. He recommends using a small area that has a wide variety of differences. For example, have students map an area that includes a trampled section as well as relatively undisturbed lawn. Or use a mowed area that adjoins an unmowed plot. The area can be divided using a string grid and students can record a variety of data that is found in each section. Sobel recommends that you have students locate specific items on their maps such as stones, dirt patches, twigs, anthills, litter, or different species of plants (1998, 74–75). Once the maps are completed, students can analyze what the maps reveal: Are certain types of plants more prevalent in one area than another? Why was more litter found in some quadrants than in others?

Whether students are making their own maps of the schoolyard or are using ones that you have developed, they are going outside and taking a closer look at the natural world. To paraphrase Sobel, by mapping a familiar area, students will discover things that had been there all along, but just had never been noticed.

Mapping with Technology

With older students, global positioning system (GPS) devices can be used to mark the locations of points of interest on the school grounds and to keep track of such things as animal homes or unusual plants. GPS devices help to develop the concept of determining location through a grid system. By downloading GPS data into mapping software, students can create a map that includes the information they have gathered concerning the local area.

Going beyond the schoolyard, GPS units can be used to mark points of historic, cultural, or economic interest in the community. One Midwest middle school teacher had his students research information about local community leaders in the early 1900s and then locate where their homes or businesses were located. The students used GPS units to mark the locations and they took digital pictures if the structures were still standing. Students then created a slide show that included the maps and pictures. The presentation generated a lot of discussion about why things are located where they are and whether or not the locations reflected patterns. The result was a far more dynamic product than if kids had just written traditional reports.

The Google Earth mapping product allows students to upload GPS data and display it on aerial maps of the local area. Most popular mapping programs from companies such as Rand McNally or DeLorme also now provide the option of uploading GPS waypoints into the maps that are produced. Seeing the data that you have collected in the field appear on a "real" map is a powerful motivator.

Using the schoolyard for mapping activities can focus on such key geography education questions as: Where are things located? Why are they located where they are? What patterns are reflected in the groupings of things?

Digs

A simulated archeological dig can be a great way to spark an interest in history. Mary Ann Albright describes an archeological dig project for elementary-age students sponsored by Oregon State University (Albright 2006). This class of middle grades students created their own archeological adventure. The group was divided into two sections; each one developed a "culture." Students then created artifacts that could represent aspects of the culture such as transportation, communication, economics, food, clothing, recreational habits, and so on.

Next, they buried the artifacts in layers, with the "oldest" items placed at the bottom. The two groups then exchanged sites and began their excavations using traditional trowels and sifters so as not to miss even the tiniest artifact. Albright notes that each group even "included a 'Rosetta Stone' and other clues for cracking their language codes." As each group found items, students recorded their locations and descriptions. The two groups then had to use their artifacts to hypothesize about the nature of the culture that was being represented.

A well-planned dig simulation can be an excellent problem-solving activity and a powerful segue into many social studies topics. It's a great way to foster discussions about people, places, and environments.

A Few More Quick Ideas

An Ohio teacher has students explore the influence of topography on water flow by taking students outside for a careful look after a heavy rain. As students explore how water flows across the school grounds, the concept of a watershed begins to emerge.

An Illinois teacher maintains a small prairie for students to plant, identify and label, and weed. It's a great way for students to get hands-on experience with the plants that used to cover the land on which their school now stands.

A Minnesota teacher suggests contacting your local historical society or library to obtain copies of journals from early settlers. It's interesting to read how these folks described the landscape. If possible, try to find descriptions of an area that you can readily locate—ideally, a location similar to where your school is located. Take the class outside, read the historic description, and discuss how things have changed.

111

Language Arts

The outdoors can serve as both venue and content as students use spoken, written, and visual language. Because the outdoors pulls at the senses, the schoolyard can provide fantastic raw material for description!

The outdoors can provide great inspiration for writing poetry. Because the outdoors stimulates thinking in so many directions, students don't have a problem finding substance for poetry writing. A very effective introduction to poetry is the "See What I Found" formula poem. This is one of those activities that has been around for many years, but I have no idea who may have "invented" it. Although this may not fit a technical description of poetry, it certainly emphasizes the aesthetic qualities of language and coaxes the use of descriptive words. The structure of this five-line poem is very simple:

First line:	See what I found?
Second line:	(name of object)
Third line:	(adjectives and/or descriptive phrase)
Fourth line:	(tell where you found it)
Fifth line:	(make a comment or question about it)

See what I found?
A butterfly
Flitting and glowing in the sunlight.
It's resting on a flower.
I wonder how long it will stay?

There are many ways to do this poetry activity. Sometimes I will have students find an object in nature that is no larger than a thumbnail. They bring the object to the outdoor teaching area and write the "See What I Found" poem. They always, then, return the natural items back to the original locations.

Another variation is to have kids take their clipboards or lapboards and find something interesting without removing it from its setting. This can be another one of those activities that can focus on either the macro or micro aspects of the schoolyard. You can have students find a special spot and then write about something no more than 3 feet away from them. Or you can have them sit on the grass and write about something they see in the distance. I really like this option since it does not disturb the environment, and makes it possible to utilize an animal or large object in the poem. It's also great to see kids enjoying the outdoors, observing and writing.

The previously described Tale of the Tape activity (Chapter 4), in which students generate a listing of adjectives and descriptive phrases for a natural object, makes a wonderful precursor to the "See What I

Found" poem. One teacher includes Tale of the Tape as an introduction to the use of the thesaurus.

The schoolyard can provide a magnificent setting for many traditional language arts activities. For example, Pam Tempest takes advantage of the Florida sunshine by frequently taking her students outside for reading. Sometimes she reads a story aloud to students outside and other times the schoolyard is used for sustained silent reading. Sometimes Pam has a small group of students who borrow a quilt and sit outside of her classroom windows on the lawn and read.

An Ohio teacher achieves a change of pace and place by taking students outside to write poetry on the sidewalk with colorful chalk. The novel setting and unconventional writing tools spur the creative juices, with nature often providing a creative writing prompt.

Since the outdoors is so conducive to reading or writing, it is well worth the effort to create an outdoor seating area. As a bonus, an outdoor courtyard or other type of outdoor seating area can also serve as a location for performance.

Language arts standards emphasize that students should be able to use spoken, written, and visual language to communicate for different purposes. In the outdoors, those purposes might include describing evidence of an environmental problem found on the school site and then researching the problem, gathering data, and proposing solutions. Or it might include describing one's own feelings and responses to the outdoors.

Interdisciplinary Use of the Outdoors

Green Journal

Fifth-grade teacher Laura Grimm has a wonderful activity that incorporates several disciplines, but is unified through the use of a journal. The Green Journal provides a vehicle for doing narrative, expository, and persuasive writing. The journal also is an activity that continues throughout the school year, thereby providing a contrast to the short-span activities that usually comprise a classroom routine. Because the journal incorporates so many elements of outdoor-enhanced learning, and is such a good example of an interdisciplinary activity, I provide the details and instructions in the following text.

113

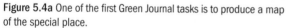

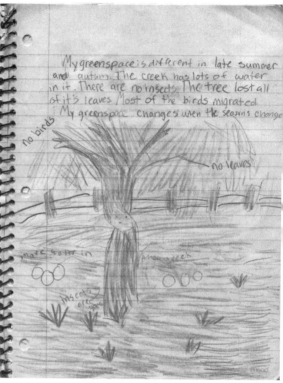

Figure 5.4a One of the first Green Journal tasks is to produce a map of the special place.

Figure 5.4b Words and pictures show changes in the special place as the seasons pass.

114

The Green Journal activity begins in the first few weeks of school. Laura provides each student with a spiral bound notebook (green cover, of course). She gives a different set of instructions each month and students paste them onto the journal pages. December and January are combined into one assignment.

In the August assignment, each student locates a special place. The area is not larger than 10 feet by 10 feet. Although Laura has students choose a spot near their homes, the various tasks and activities could also be done using a location on the school grounds, similar to the "sit area" concept described previously. Students then describe their special place in words and pictures, as shown in Figures 5.4a and b.

Here are the themes and a few sample activities from Laura's instructions to her students each month. Notice the wide range of activities and content areas that are incorporated.

September Theme: Classifying

- List at least fifteen things found in your special place.
- Make a table to classify them as living, nonliving, or once living.
- Make a bar graph or pictograph to share your results.
- Write your own definition of the following: living, nonliving, once living.

October Theme: Mapping and Measurement

- Draw a map of your special place.
- Include a key, compass rose, measurement scale, and draw from a "bird's-eye view."

November Theme: Comparing and Contrasting Seasonal Change

- Make detailed observations (words and pictures) about your special place now that autumn has arrived. Has anything changed? Do you notice anything new? Is anything missing?
- Make a Venn diagram to help you organize your thoughts.
- Write a paragraph to compare and contrast late summer and autumn as they relate to your special place.
- Illustrate your paragraph.

December/January Theme: Recording Data and Making Predictions

- Make observations, measurements, and draw pictures about the weather.
- At the end of January, write a summary of December and January's weather.
- What do the plants and animals in your special place do to survive the winter? (This may require some research.) Predict what will happen to the living things in your special place if you have an especially "hard" winter.

February Theme: Needs of Living Things

- Identify the items in your special place that provide plants and animals with what they need in order to live. You may do this in a table, drawing, or paragraph.
- Make a mini poster for your journal that advertises your special place as a great place for animals and plants to live. Be sure to include the basic needs of living things.

115

March Theme: Water Cycle and Hypothesis

- Draw and label how the water cycle might occur in your place
- Make a hypothesis as to what would happen to your specia place following a heavy rainstorm. If a heavy rainstorm occurs make observations to see if your hypothesis was correct.
- Make a hypothesis as to what would happen to your specia place in a drought.

April Theme: Signs of Spring and Your Senses

- Use your senses to observe and describe spring's arrival.
- At the beginning of the month, predict what changes wil take place in your place during the month of April. Record your predictions in the journal. At the end of the month, make observations to see if your predictions were true.

May Theme: Reflection and Evaluation

- Take someone with you to your special place. Read your Green Journal to him or her. Show your pictures, graphs, and tables
- Reflect on all that you have done this year with your Green Journal. Was it a good activity? How might it be improved?
- Write a letter to the teacher that includes the following:

What did you think about keeping a Green Journal?

- What did you like most?
- What did you like least?
- Discuss three things you learned by keeping your journal.
- Do you have any suggestions for next year?
- How might you have improved your journal?

Although the Green Journal is a great interdisciplinary activity, the major side benefit is the opportunity it provides for a child to develop a connection with a special place near home. Richard Louv, author of *Last Child in the Woods,* notes that "many of us can remember the small galaxies that we adopted as children, the slope behind the neighborhood, the strand of trees at the end of the cul-de-sac" (2005, 171).

My own "small galaxy" was an old apple tree in a field behind our house. Although the tree was a neighborhood social center, I also considered it to be my personal spot since I could see it from my backyard and quickly climb it when no one else was around. It was one of those wonderful old trees that had big branches low enough or easy climbing and perfect for just lounging with your back resting against the sturdy old trunk. That tree definitely would have been the focal point of my Green Journal.

I watched the seasons change from my perch, but my memories now are not of spring blossoms or fall leaves. Rather, I can still feel the sense of calm mingled with a feeling of groundedness that came from finding a place in nature that I considered special. Laura Grimm's Green Journal activity gives students an opportunity to nurture that same sense of personal space in nature.

Other Areas of the Curriculum

Schoolyard-enhanced learning is adaptable to most any area of the curriculum. If we think of the outdoors as both venue and content, the opportunities are limitless. The foreign language teacher can benefit from a change of pace and place by taking students outside to learn the names of natural objects in the target language. The family and consumer science teacher can have students grow fresh herbs so they can experience that not everything needs to be poured from a box. Industrial technology classes can improve the school site by constructing seating or adding enhancements such as feeders and nesting boxes to the school grounds.

The fine arts can also use the schoolyard extensively as both venue and content. Sitting outside on a beautiful spring afternoon can inspire artistic expression in a group of fourth graders, just as it has motivated artists over the centuries. Abstract concepts such as hue, shading, and texture become more concrete when actually spotted in the outdoors. A variety of nature-related crafts can be created from the abundance of natural materials found even on a small schoolyard.

An outdoor setting can provide a perfect venue for playing or creating music. How logical and powerful to teach a song about nature while actually being in nature! Students can be encouraged to create song lyrics inspired by both the micro and the macro elements of their natural surroundings. Creative movement and dance activities also blend harmoniously into an outdoor setting.

The key to effective use of the schoolyard in any curricular area is to think of the outdoors in terms of both content and venue. Ask yourself first if the outdoors can provide examples, specimens, or experiences that relate directly to the *content* of a lesson. However, even when the content may not be directly outdoor related or supported keep looking for possibilities to use the schoolyard as a *venue* for learning—opportunities to incorporate a change of pace and place. Students of any age appreciate a change of routine. Teachers, also, are energized when new settings are used to present traditional concepts. Give it a try!

Chapter 6
Beyond the Schoolyard

"I've never heard it this quiet before."

—Ari

As an eighth grader, Ari participated in an "Outdoor Adventures Day" field trip organized by his science teacher. Students spent the day doing traditional camp activities such as hiking, campfire cooking, and geocaching. Ari made this wonderful reflection while looking for a geocache on top of a rock formation.

It's thought provoking that the absence of noise would have such an impact on a fourteen-year-old who had been in the outdoors for only a few hours. But it's certainly understandable. Electronic beeps, ring tones, the incessant babble of the television steadily assault our eardrums. Even the car has become an electronic noise zone with hands-free calling, satellite radio, and on-board DVD systems. The statement "I've never heard it this quiet before" is perhaps more of a plea than an observation.

The outdoors is not a quiet place to those who have learned to listen to nature. The gentle sound of a breeze nudging pine branches, the intricate melodies of bird calls, and the soothing white noise of insects buzzing on a summer afternoon affirm that nature is never really still. Unfortunately, those sounds are very foreign to many youth today. If children are to ever listen in to the natural world, they need to be nurtured through opportunity and example.

I believe that a critical role of schools in children's lives is to include experiences and opportunities that encourage careful listening and provide rich exposure to environments and vibrant locations that reinforce what kids learn in classrooms. In previous chapters we have explored ways to make maximum use of the environment in the schoolyard. If you develop a pattern of frequently using schoolyard-enhanced learning experiences, students become accustomed to the procedures and behavior expectations that you have for outdoor learning.

By utilizing the school grounds regularly as both a venue and source of content, parents, colleagues, and administrators also begin to accept outdoor instruction as a regular part of your teaching repertoire. The need to defend outdoor teaching becomes less and less of a concern, and you'll be able to creatively expand your use of the schoolyard.

The occasional field trip or a more extended outdoor adventure can provide additional learning experiences that would be impossible to do only in a schoolyard. For instance, you can begin to develop the idea of a habitat with examples on the schoolyard, but a trip to a forest or marsh can provide vivid images and experiences that will solidify the concept. When students are already accustomed to outdoor learning activities at school, there is no need to spend time acclimating kids into an outdoor learning routine—they already understand your expectations and have accepted experiential learning as a part of your teaching style.

This chapter provides a variety of possibilities for building upon and extending schoolyard–enhanced learning experiences. We explore topics such as ways to make traditional hikes engaging, how to incorporate GPS technology into both schoolyard and off-site experiences, and techniques for utilizing the outdoors for team-building and problem-solving tasks. A section about resident outdoor education, or school camping, is also included for those who are interested in more comprehensive outdoor experiences for their students.

Making the Most of a Hike

A field trip to a local park or nearby nature preserve can help students explore an accessible outdoor resource in their own community. It may also encourage families to return to the locale for their own outings. Leading a hike with a group of students presents unique challenges, though.

Taking a class away for a field trip of any kind always requires careful advance planning. A trip to a park, however, is more complex than a visit to an indoor location such as a museum or science center. You determine the schedule, route, and learning activities for the visit —a more complex task than simply stepping off the bus and turning the group over to a staff member at a facility. A field trip to a park also adds the need for greater emphasis on classroom management since students may not have clearly visible boundaries and can readily start exploring in all directions.

Field trips that include trail hikes can be great learning experiences. A trek in the forest can provide sights, sounds, and smells that may be new and intriguing to many techno-saturated kids. The trail provides a natural progression for learning activities by providing examples of content previously taught in the classroom. But, a good hike should be much more than a quick dash through the woods. Most problems occur when teachers assume that kids will be focused and fascinated as they walk the trail. Although the teacher may be intrigued by every berry and bug along the way, it's prudent to remember that most students are not yet at that same level of appreciation. Children need focusing activities to keep their minds aligned with the objectives of the hike. Several years of hiking with kids have generated some cautions and procedures that I try to follow faithfully and share with you here.

Before the Hike

Determine the Focus

The general goal of "enjoying nature" is noble and certainly an overarching purpose, but hikes with kids go better when there is a more specific objective in mind. What are the main concepts that kids should take with them after the hike? Perhaps it's diversity in nature, or habitats, or erosion; or maybe it's an appreciation of shape and texture in the outdoors. The concepts you choose to emphasize will be driven primarily by your curriculum, but also by previous learning activities that you did at school and now want to reinforce on the hike. For example, the mini-habitats you examined on the school grounds provide a great background for exploring more complex habitats in a forest.

In keeping with today's standards-driven environment, there need to be a curricular linkage to justify school time and money for an off-site experience. Field trips can provide an excellent anticipatory set or "hook" to launch a new unit of study. For example, an ecology unit can repeatedly build on observations and activities that were made during an initial field trip to a nature preserve. Digital pictures of the trip can provide a great library of examples that are very relevant since the students actually were there.

Trips also can work very effectively as capstone or closure experiences to units of study. A Virginia social studies teacher culminates a unit about the Civil War by taking students first to the local historical society and then to a historic cemetery. Students learn from the historians about local people who served in the Civil War. Students see artifacts from these soldiers and often can read excerpts from their diaries. The next stop is the cemetery where students are able to find many of the tombstones of the soldiers they learned about. When possible, tombstone rubbings are carefully made and brought back to the classroom. The locations of the stones are also recorded using GPS devices so that a map can be constructed later. The field trip has a powerful impact as students quickly realize that abstract terms such as *casualties* and *soldiers* refer to real people whose words they have read and whose personal possessions they have seen.

Scout the Trail in Advance

If you will be the hike leader, it is essential that you walk the entire trail within a week or two of your visit. You need to know what will be around the next bend. That great trail you took a year ago may have suffered considerable storm damage, or vandals may have left some nasty stuff along the way, or some of your favorite points of interest may have been removed or damaged.

Explain the Trail Rules

This needs to be done first at the school and then repeated again at the trailhead. Like all classroom rules, keep them simple and easy to translate into behavior. Many kids today have had very limited hiking experience and truly do not have a concept of trail etiquette. You may want to stress such things as:

- Stay with the group and don't get ahead of the leader or behind the adult at the end of the line.

122

- Practice a signal like a raised hand to quickly get the group's attention.
- Point out that other groups may also be in the area, so yelling would be distracting to both people and animals.
- Discuss conservation considerations: Leave wildflowers, plants, and branches where they are (i.e., don't, pick, pull, yank or defoliate!).
- Stay on the trail and try not to disturb the natural setting. Explain to kids that hillsides erode rapidly and vegetation is quickly destroyed if people frequently get off the trail.

Early in the Hike

Many folks view a hike as simply a duty-bound quest to be accomplished: "Let's get from point A to point B and hope that some nature appreciation seeps in." Nature hikes can be so much more than just brisk walks down a path. Take advantage of the fact that student anticipation is at its highest right before the hike begins. Capitalize on children's natural curiosity about new surroundings by providing a little preview of what might be around the bend.

Try to capture student interest even before starting to hike. While still at the trailhead, use something tangible—a natural object or a historical artifact related to the area—that will generate curiosity.

I like to show kids samples of bedstraw, a plant that is sometimes referred to as "nature's Velcro," since it has tiny spines on the leaves and stems that readily stick to clothing. Kids are intrigued as a sprig of the plant is tossed on a shirt and immediately sticks. After everyone has had a chance to try it, I explain that bedstraw was sometimes used years ago to form pillows or sleeping mats since the stems readily stick together and form a resilient pad.

Historical background can also set the stage for a hike. One teacher shows examples of Native American tools and arrowheads that would have been common in her area. A lively discussion can evolve about the types of animals that must have been roaming in the park centuries ago.

During the Hike

The secret to making a hike both engaging and educational is to incorporate a heavy dose of variety. The formula that works well for me is to hike with the group for five to ten minutes then do an activity;

123

hike for another five to ten minutes; do an activity . . . hike . . . activity
The entire time on the trail alternates between walking and doing
brief activities.

For example, some activities described in Chapter 5—"Nature
Analogies," "A Closer Look," "Nanohike," and some noninvasive
scavenger hunts—are well suited to a trail hike. They all are activities
that require minimal materials that can be easily tucked in a day pack.
By using a pattern of hike and focus you constantly keep kids alert to
their surroundings.

Another effective activity is the drop-off hike. As you walk along,
drop off kids one at a time at points of interest that you see along
the trail. The stations can be a mix of natural history facts as well
as interesting observations. For example, have students pointing out
such things as poison ivy, fungi, plants of unusual color or shape,
signs of animal activity, an unusual leaf, indications of erosion, or bark
textures. The child stands at his spot and points out the interesting
item to all who walk by. After all have passed, the child joins the line
again and hears the other points of interest. This very simple activity
involves everyone and has tremendous appeal since each student
serves as the "expert" for a point of interest.

It's helpful to bring along some simple plant and animal
identification guides. A digital camera also is a great way to capture
interesting features and critters for future analysis. There always are
students who are interested in knowing the name of a particular plant
or animal. I feel that students learn greater appreciation for nature
when both student and teacher eagerly try to find out the name of
something that was found outdoors.

After the Hike

As soon as the hike ends, take some time to debrief the experience.
Simple questions can start some good discussions:

What was the most unusual thing we saw?

Did we see anything on the hike that we also see on our school
grounds?

Did you see something on the hike that you didn't expect to see?

These questions really help to emphasize the value of the hiking
experience. Students usually mention animals that were spotted along
the way, although plants sometimes make the unexpected list. I like
to include a time during the hike when students just sit quietly apart

from each other for a few minutes. That's when the bold bird lands on a nearby branch, or a little critter scampers across the trail. Although rarely seen by a group of tromping students, toads and garter snakes cause the greatest excitement as both the most unusual and the most unexpected encounters on a hike here in the North!

It's most effective to debrief the hike while you are still on the site. Impressions are very fresh and enthusiasm is high. The debriefing time brings closure to the hike and helps kids to sort out the experiences that they had.

When back at the school, try to plan something that ties in with the hike experience. It might be drawing, creative writing, or using collected data in a math activity lesson. For example, as the hike begins, give students a sheet with pictures of tree species they will pass on the trail. Students mark the sheet every time they pass one of the trees. Back at the school, they use the data to compute the average number of each species on the trail and draw charts to illustrate the findings. Another way to link the hike with school is to use the GPS devices described in the next section to track the route of the hike and also mark points of interest. This information can then be downloaded back at the school and printed. A writing activity can then be framed around the points of interest that were chosen as waypoints.

The GPS as a Teaching Tool

Wouldn't it be wonderful to have a technological gizmo that actually encourages kids to go outside, rather than stare passively at a screen? The paradox of nature blending with electronics is not only possible, but also provides various teaching tools. Global Positioning System (GPS) devices are intriguing gadgets that combine the technological feel that kids are so accustomed to, with enriching outdoor experiences (see Figure 6.1).

One unique way to bring data back to the classroom is to take GPS devices along on the field trip. The GPS can help you to re-create your route and points of interest back at the school.

Figure 6.1 GPS devices provide an excellent way to blend technology with the outdoors. The ability to record exact locations of outdoor points of interest makes possible a variety of instructional activities.

GPS units are certainly not toys. The GPS is a sophisticated radio navigation system that allows users to determine accurate location, velocity, and time twenty-four hours a day, anywhere in the world. GPS devices are popping up everywhere, from delivery trucks to cell phones. They are a mainstay for construction and surveying, and increasingly are being found even in the family car.

For many years, GPS units were too expensive for school use. However, increasing demand and advancing technology have made these versatile devices accessible to schools. GPS devices of adequate sophistication for middle and high school use are now available at discount stores for less than 90 dollars. Since classroom GPS projects can be easily designed for groups of two or three students, only seven or eight units would be needed for an average class. Although the cost is still significant, the purchasing of a classroom set may be a project that a parent organization would be willing to fund. One set of units centrally stored in a resource center could readily serve an entire building.

The ability of a GPS device to pinpoint a location (often referred to as a waypoint), and then store the coordinates for future reference, makes it a very useful tool for school projects. Students can locate interesting specimens or artifacts in the schoolyard or community, mark the waypoints with the press of a button, and then reenter the coordinates and return to those exact locations months or even years later. Changes can be analyzed, locations of important examples can be stored for future use, maps can be developed, or presentations prepared.

Learning Benefits of GPS Devices

Outdoor Experiences

First and foremost, the GPS device takes kids into the outdoors. I strongly believe that if you can just get kids outside, you increase the possibility that they may see, hear, smell, or touch something that will help them to connect with nature.

Hands-On and Technology-Based Learning

GPS devices include many electronic features that are familiar to kids. The screens, scrolling features, and multifunctional buttons are very familiar to today's techno-savvy kids. Handheld GPS units are intriguing to students since the devices are still not common enough to be found in the average home. I have found that students are captivated with the challenge of exploring yet another electronic gadget.

Great Segue into Other Technologies

Probably the most powerful pairing is the digital camera with the GPS. There are many software programs available that make it very easy to pair a waypoint with a digital picture. It then is possible to print out maps that show a picture taken at each waypoint. What a great way to document interesting sites and also to present information to a class. The pictures and maps presented can easily be included in PowerPoint presentations.

GPS data can also be uploaded into products such as Google Earth, the powerful, virtual globe program that provides maps of the earth based on satellite and aerial photos. Seeing local data in the context of a much larger scale can open many opportunities for dialogue. Students can use the program's zoom capabilities to see if similar topography is close by, to speculate why certain features or historic structures were placed in specific locations, or to trace the routes of streams and creeks.

Students can do even more in-depth analysis when GPS data is integrated with Geographic Information Systems (GIS) that permit the creation of highly specialized maps by adding and manipulating layers of data. GIS provides the powerful capability to overlay nearly any type of data that has been collected for an area. Students can then ponder what types of relationships exist between their data and its intersection with other GIS data layers that have been imported.

Since effective use of GIS requires an understanding of map terminology, the meaning of data sets, and the abstract concept of data layering, it is most often utilized at the middle and high school levels. However, even some elementary schools are giving GIS a try.

Autumn Phillips describes how second and fourth graders in Hayden, Colorado, marked roadkill locations with GPS devices and then used GIS software to plot the data on a map of U.S. Highway 40 (2003). In the valley where the school is located, there is a stretch of Highway 40 that had been the site of numerous roadkills and automobile accidents as deer and other wildlife crossed the road in search of water and food. Students collected data with the help of community members and examined it using GIS software. Students created a map that ran the length of a hallway and showed the locations of roadkill and natural features in the area. The data provided useful information for the Colorado Division of Wildlife, and most important, helped students see real-life applications of math,

127

science, and problem-solving. What a great example of place-based education in action!

Higher-Order Thinking Skills

Students develop the ability to gather and then map data, combined with the capability of returning to exact locations for further analysis. This makes it possible to pose a variety of questions that go beyond the simple recall of facts. The use of GPS devices also models for students how technology can be used to gather the data needed to answer questions and solve problems. Since the GPS device can facilitate the tracking of information over time, robust data sets can be collected that provide opportunities for speculation about changes that emerge. Teacher questions can encourage real data analysis and speculation, rather than merely factual recall:

"From the data, identify a trend."

"Based on what you found, identify a problem."

"What might have caused the changes seen over time?"

"What changes might we see the next time we go out?"

Useful in a Variety of Content Areas

The power of the GPS comes from its capability to mark locations of objects, events, specimens, landmarks—anything that would be useful to recall or revisit. Since information can be downloaded from GPS devices, it is easy to create maps of the area with the points of interest clearly marked. This visual representation of data, coupled with the ability to return to an exact location, can provide the impetus for discussion and analysis in several content areas. Following are some examples.

Science

Mark and map the location of animal homes on the school site. Have students discuss why there appear to be certain clusterings of animal homes.

Mark and map examples of erosion on the school site or in the community. Use topographic maps to explore possible causes for the erosion.

One school planted a variety of spring flower bulbs in the fall. Students recorded the locations with GPS devices and then downloaded the locations into a map. For each location, students listed the type of bulb planted and the expected color of the bloom. In the spring, students went to the exact locations and recorded what actually happened. They discussed which species of plants seemed to be the most successful and speculated why some bulbs didn't produce plants.

Another school near a wooded area used GPS devices to record locations of spring wildflowers. Their locations were mapped and photographed so that the next year's class could locate the specimens.

Social Studies

Mark, map, and photograph historic locations in the community. This is a great activity to do in conjunction with a local historical society. One class actually helped the society prepare a community heritage brochure complete with photos to distribute in the community.

Use the devices to make the abstract concepts of latitude and longitude more concrete. After discussing these terms indoors, have students load specific latitude and longitude coordinates into the GPS and find destinations on the school grounds. By making a grid of the school grounds, you can show students how the GPS is actually showing the intersection of two coordinates.

Mark and map where certain types of stores or services are located in a community and hypothesize why certain patterns have evolved.

Math

Using the altitude function of the GPS, have students verify the data shown on topographic maps that include the school grounds.

Since GPS devices show distance traveled as well as speed, the devices can provide another way to illustrate measurement concepts.

Language Arts

Build an expository writing activity around the concept of geocaching. First, have

Pizza Geography

To introduce National Geography Standard III– "How to analyze the spatial organization of people, places, and environments on Earth's surface"–Massachusetts teacher Donna LaRoche contributed an engaging lesson titled the "Geography of Pizza' to the National Geographic lesson plan site (2006). The lesson serves as a great introduction to the concept of points, lines, and areas; I have used it as a segue into the use of the GPS. Instead of marking points by hand, we can do it electronically with a GPS device and also use the tracklog feature to record routings.

The lesson has students locate local pizza shops in a phone book and then plot their locations on a map. They also mark their homes and the school on the same map. Students use the data to draw a route from the school to the nearest pizzeria, as well as routes from their homes to a nearby pizza shop. Students analyze whether alternate routes are feasible and what would be the logical "neighborhood" from which the restaurant would draw customers.

students research the activity. Next, have kids actually put together their own cache for the school grounds. The main writing task is then to develop a brochure describing geocaching, the type of cache that has been established on the school site, and how to use a GPS to find the cache.

My son, Matthew, and his wife, Kristin, have merged poetry and GPS. The activity is based upon the development of two-line poems crafted in a form described by author Sheila Bender:

> At the heart of a poet's ability to evoke engagement with experience is the use of metaphor to make images come alive. With metaphor, the poet compares one thing to something else that is very different. The juxtaposition makes the writer re-experience the original image more fully. In Africa, the people of the Bantu tribe developed an oral tradition in which they did this. They created two-line poems in the rhythm of their work. The first line was an image spoken by one person and the second line an "answering" or corresponding image spoken by a second person. (Bender)

Matthew gives each pair of students a clipboard, blank paper, pencil, and a GPS device. Students write their names and GPS device number at the top of the paper. The next steps are as follows.

1) He asks each pair to go to a location on the school grounds that provides inspiration or interest. The location is marked as a waypoint on the GPS and one student creates the first line of the poem based upon the surroundings (e.g., the smell of a decaying log). The second student then completes the second line. Here are two examples:

> The smell of a decaying log.
> An old book found in a trunk.

or

> The sound of fall leaves shuffling underfoot.
> Waves crashing on the shore.

2) After completing the second line, the students fold over the top of the paper, covering the completed poem. They then return to the meeting area and trade both the GPS unit and the corresponding paper with another pair.

3) The new pair then uses the GPS to locate the inspiration location, examines the area, and completes a new two-line poem. The new poem is also folded under and the pair returns to the meeting area.

4) Depending on the number of pairs and available time, this exchange process can continue for several more rounds. Poems and GPS units are traded and the process is repeated with the new poem always folded under and hidden from view.

5) After several rounds, everyone returns to the meeting area and poems are returned to the original authors. A variety of activities can follow:

   - Students may share the poems in small groups.
   - Students may show each other the various locations and read the poems there.
   - Waypoints can be uploaded and maps created with a favorite poem being placed at each point on the map.

This activity is very effective with older students. The GPS units add novelty and interest to a language arts activity that combines careful outdoor observation with a good exposure to the power of metaphor.

Getting Started with the GPS

Students need to understand that the GPS device helps us to find specific locations on the earth, just like a map helps us to pinpoint a particular place. I always begin by talking about the concept of latitude and longitude, and have students look at two-dimensional examples of grids, both on paper and on the classroom floor, to visualize how the intersection of the lines determines a point. Talking about the point defined by the intersection of two streets can be a good way to make the concept more concrete. An excellent overview of latitude and longitude stated in kid-friendly terms can be found at the Journey North site (http://www.learner.org/jnorth/tm/LongitudeIntro.html) referred to in the "Resources" section.

After an explanation of how the GPS uses satellites to determine location, I then distribute the devices while we are still in the classroom. We practice using the various screens and functions of the GPS and then move outside to try a few practice activities that help students become familiar with the devices. The following activities have been my mainstays for helping students to practice and develop confidence using a GPS unit.

GPS Hold 'Em

After grouping students in pairs, have them form a circle in a large, open area and face outward. Give each pair a playing card and a numbered GPS device. The pairs walk straight ahead for forty or fifty paces, drop the card, and mark the spot as a waypoint. Everyone returns to the circle and exchanges GPS units along with a description of the playing card that is located at that waypoint. The pairs do a "go to" with the GPS and are off to see if they can find the correct card.

This activity works very well, even with first-time users of GPS equipment. I emphasize to the pairs that they shouldn't try to completely hide the cards; enough of the card should be showing so that it can be spotted when another pair gets reasonably close.

Color Scavenger Hunt

This activity expands on GPS Hold 'Em by requiring students to locate multiple waypoints in a sequence. Each pair of students has three sheets of paper of a distinctive color. The pairs go out and hide the paper, marking a waypoint each time. The pairs then return to the circle, exchange GPS devices, and set off to find the three locations that have been marked.

Treasure Trail Scavenger Hunt

For this activity, you set up and store a predetermined set of waypoints into the GPS devices. Inexpensive items such as erasers, pencils, or stickers can be placed in plastic containers at the various locations. As students locate each destination, they gather an item from the cache. Another variation is to have an envelope with a question placed at each waypoint. Questions usually refer to the immediate surroundings, such as "What tall object is very close to you?" (flagpole), "What man-made object is helping animals?" (bird feeder). Students record their answers on a tally sheet so that you can confirm successful location of the waypoints.

These three activities are intended to give students an opportunity to experiment with the GPS unit and become familiar with its operation. After doing these activities, students should be ready to use the devices as a part of instructional activities.

When kids become comfortable with a GPS, you can show them that they have been simulating an activity commonly referred to as geocaching—an electronic treasure hunt using GPS devices. Direct them to http://www.geocaching.com, a comprehensive website that thoroughly explains this wonderful, family-friendly adventure game that has cache locations worldwide. Almost every North American town is within a few miles of a geocache. Geocaching is an amazingly simple, yet highly engaging, activity that gets entire families back into nature and into communication with each other.

Many of the GPS activities described here involve elements of teamwork and group problem-solving. Using the GPS for scavenger hunts or geocaching requires that the group work together to interpret directions, input data, and look carefully for visual clues. These types of

Practical Tips for Using the GPS in the Classroom

A few thoughts to keep in mind as you consider the GPS as a teaching tool:

· You do not need a GPS unit for each student. Students do just fine working in pairs if you emphasize that they will have to take turns with the devices. Trios will work also, but pairs provide everyone with more individual time to operate the units.

· Be sure to number the units with a permanent marker. It makes it much easier to keep track of the units when they are exchanged in activities.

· You do not need an expensive GPS unit for typical school applications. Most low-end machines will work fine. It's critical, though, that the units have download capability. To maximize the educational value of the GPS, you need to be able to plug the device into your computer so that your data can be used in a variety of applications. Although most units produced today have that capability, it is very helpful if the download cable uses a USB connector into your computer. Non-USB connectors often can't connect to laptops, which requires the purchase of special adaptors. Check out the type of cable and whether it is compatible with the computer you will be using for downloading.

· It's helpful to have mapping software loaded into your computer. Most of the major brand-name mapping programs allow you to download waypoints and tracks from a GPS unit.

· Although not usually necessary, a GPS unit that contains a base map can be useful. The base map enables you to show your waypoints in terms of the roads in your area right on the GPS screen.

· Be sure that all devices are turned off at the end of a session. Most units intentionally do not shut off automatically (you wouldn't want that to happen on the trail!), so batteries can be drained quickly if they are accidentally left on while in storage. Battery replacement is the only real recurring expense with GPS units.

· Stress safety. Emphasize to students that GPS units indicate a route "as the crow flies." In other words, the unit will not warn you that there is a building, large tree, or busy road directly in the path that is indicated. Students need to understand that they may have to deviate from the route indicated on the machine in order to get around an obstacle.

activities use the outdoors as a venue to reinforce group process skills, and fall into a general category often referred to as *initiative tasks*.

Initiative Tasks

Although the term sounds complex, the concept is really quite simple. Initiative tasks are structured activities designed to develop leadership skills, a sense of team/group identity, and group problem-solving skills. On the surface, initiatives simply look like creative games. When done correctly, however, with careful debriefing after the activity, initiatives can produce lasting changes in group dynamics. For that reason, many corporations spend large amounts of money on team-building seminars, which usually are centered around a series of initiative task activities. Initiatives can be equally useful in establishing and maintaining a feeling of unity within a classroom.

The initiative may be as simple as having everyone line up by birthday without talking, or as complex as putting together a structure without knowing what the end product will look like or working together to move your group across a ropes course 40 feet in the air.

There are both low- and high-order initiatives. Low-order tasks use simple equipment and usually keep people on the ground. For example, solving the problem of how to get a group across a given distance using only some boards and tin cans, or having a group hold onto a rope circle and form various shapes while blindfolded would be types of low-order initiatives.

Higher-order initiatives involve elaborate props and equipment, complex procedures, elements of physical challenge, and may even include aerial elements including elevated ropes courses. Examples would be getting a group over a high climbing wall, or moving everyone through a simulated giant rope spiderweb without touching a strand. Higher-order initiatives should only be led by persons who have been thoroughly trained in both equipment and methodology. There is frequently a need for spotters since many high-order initiatives involve physical activity.

There are many low order initiatives that are very appropriate for use on the school grounds. All initiatives, whether high- or low-order, have the leader follow the same general sequence.

Present a Problem or Task

Since the task often involves the movement of an object or the entire group from one place to another, initiatives are frequently done outdoors. The type of problem presented depends on several factors: how well the participants know each other, existing levels of trust and cooperativeness in the group, age and gender mix, physical limitations of participants, and so on.

When using initiative tasks at a school, start with a very simple, low-risk task first. The easy task sets a positive tone and makes everyone feel comfortable. Then move to something a bit more complex.

Camp directors Jerry Dunlap and his son, Trevor, stress the concept of progression when using initiative tasks. The Dunlaps emphasize "frontloading"—embedding a heavy dose of positive norms and expectations from the outset. The "no put-downs" rule is emphasized with zero tolerance for unkind remarks.

The initiative tasks they include in their camp programs move from low emotional intensity to higher levels of intensity. For example, a low-intensity task might be an ice breaker activity such as a "Find someone who . . ." scavenger hunt in which kids go around the group seeing who might fit a certain category. There is very little emotional risk-taking involved.

Next, the progression may move to a medium-intensity-level task such as having kids each hold lengths of PVC pipe and pass a marble through all the pipes and move toward an end goal. In this activity, each person feels a responsibility for making the task happen, but if the marble drops, it's not dramatic nor does it call great attention to any one person.

The Dunlaps then may progress to a high-intensity activity in which the group has to find a way to stand on a low, but small, platform. The emotional risk is elevated since it's very obvious if someone is not cooperating. In addition, the activity adds the elements of closer physical proximity and agility.

In a school setting, you probably won't be doing tasks above the medium-intensity level. An activity doesn't have to be dramatic or physically risky to have an impact. The important thing is to pose a problem that doesn't have a simple answer and then let kids work it out. What makes an initiative task powerful is the "no-put-downs" atmosphere and the debriefing experience that comes later.

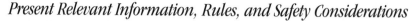

Present Relevant Information, Rules, and Safety Considerations

Safety is of prime concern. Choose activities that fit the age, temperament, and abilities of your students. An active movement-based activity may have worked great with last year's class, but with this year's group, a more subdued construction task with PVC pipes might be more appropriate. Make sure that boundaries are understood and stress the rules that must be followed.

Keep the progression concept in mind also. Find a variety of low-, medium-, and higher-level activities to keep in your files. If you find yourself weighing whether or not an activity might be too risky, don't do it! There are hundreds of other ones out there.

Step Back and Allow the Group to Approach the Problem

Hopefully, there is open discussion. But, regardless, the leader does not interject suggestions or leading questions. In this phase, the leader is just an observer, only answering questions pertaining to interpretations of the rules or guidelines. For teachers, this is a very difficult phase. We are so used to helping, coaxing, and coaching that it really is difficult to just stand back and watch a group struggle with a task.

Competition between groups is usually not encouraged in initiatives. The focus is on the group trying to improve its own time or in some other way competing against itself. Mixing intergroup competition with initiative tasks can muddy the group processes that you are trying to enhance.

When doing initiatives that involve some type of physical activity such as running or balancing, there is always the possibility that a student may feel reluctant to try the activity. Obviously, a reluctant participant should never be coaxed, either verbally or physically, to do an activity. If a positive feeling of trust has been effectively frontloaded, the student may give it a try. Be prepared, though, to give a graceful "out" for the reluctant participant. Ask the individual to help you act as a spotter or to assist you with equipment or another task related to the activity. The Dunlaps emphasize the concept of "challenge by choice," which simply means that an individual takes part in an activity only to the point that he or she feels comfortable.

Refocus the Problem when Necessary

If the group becomes hopelessly stymied, sometimes you'll need to give a hint or suggestion. The hint should be rather vague so that the group still has to wrestle a bit to complete the task.

Even after a lot of sincere effort, some groups may simply not be able to solve the task. Some purists feel that no help should be given to a group—if the group fails, so be it.

Failure to complete a task is really not a "bad" outcome. In the next phase (debriefing), there is an opportunity to analyze why the group was not able to solve the task. Frequently, even greater learning occurs when a group does an in-depth analysis of a failed attempt, rather than always applauding a success.

Conclude with a Group Discussion

The debriefing phase is the most important element of an initiative task. It's crucial to remember that this reflective phase is what makes the initiative task a learning experience rather than just a game. Watch the clock carefully so that you can provide an adequate amount of time to debrief the task. Time requirements vary based upon the complexity of the activity and the size of the group. I schedule a minimum of fifteen minutes for any initiative, but groups may spend half an hour or more on complex higher-order tasks.

Beginning the Debriefing

To begin a debriefing session, I like to move the group to a comfortable location that is in reasonable proximity to where the task took place. Being able to see the site and equipment can jog memories and elicit more specific responses. If possible, have the group sit in a circle to avoid the "leader-respondent" tone.

Establish basic ground rules for the debriefing:
- There can be no put-downs.
- You can pass on any question.
- Use the positive rather than the negative: "It might have helped if . . ." rather than "John didn't help when he . . ."

The Power of Initiative Tasks

Longtime outdoor educator Jerry Dunlap tells the story of a high school group that was attempting a climbing wall initiative at his camp. The wall was 8 feet high and the objective was to get the entire group over the wall. To accomplish the task, 100 percent cooperation was essential.

As the group began discussing a strategy for solving the task, one teenager adamantly refused to take part. Interestingly, this boy was outgoing, athletic, and strong—certainly much more physically capable of doing the task than several others in the group. As the group began to nag and criticize, Jerry firmly reiterated the "no-put-down" rule.

As the group's tone changed from belittling to focusing on why the boy was reluctant to climb the wall, he began share a traumatic incident with his peers. As a child, he had been injured in a fall from a hayloft, and had retained a fear of heights ever since. A hush came over the group as he told his story and everyone realized that this macho young athlete was really reflecting the stark reality that we all harbor concealed fears. The dynamic of the group immediately changed from taunting to encouraging. Through gentle affirmation and positive feedback, this teenager was helped by his peers not only to climb a wall, but to overcome a fear that had festered for years.

Plan Questions Beforehand

Debriefing questions are important and really should be planned in advance. Many debriefing sessions get hopelessly bogged down in one dimension and miss the opportunity for the group to examine a situation from a variety of perspectives. Many books have been written concerning debriefing and reflection. An excellent and concise read is *Lasting Lessons: A Teacher's Guide to Reflecting on Experience* by Clifford E. Knapp.

A great framework for questioning was devised by A. J. A Binker, who developed a category system of six types of questions that can help us look at a problem from many different dimensions. Here are his categories and some of his examples (Paul and Binker 1990). I have added a few comments in italics that relate to initiative tasks.

Questions of Clarification

Could you give me an example (*of cooperation that took place during the activity*)?

Let me see if I understand you; do you mean _____ or _____?

Questions That Probe Assumptions

What are you assuming?

You seem to be assuming (*that the group was not taking the task seriously*). Do I understand you correctly?

Questions That Probe Reasons and Evidence

What would be an example (*of where a suggestion was not considered*)?

What are your reasons for saying that (*the task was impossible*).

Questions About Viewpoints and Perspectives

Can/did anyone see this another way?

What is an alternative (*way to solve the task*)?

Questions That Probe Implications and Consequences

When you say (*that John was the leader*), are you implying (*that no one else was helping*)?

What effect would (*Sarah's idea*) have had?

Questions About the Questions

Is this question easy or hard to answer? Why?

To answer this question (*Why weren't more people giving suggestions?*), what questions would we have to answer first?

One experiential educator shared with me his favorite debriefing question: "What can you take away from this experience?" That really says it all.

Additional Resources

The "Resources" section of this book includes websites and an excellent book that provide directions for initiative tasks. Typing *team-building activities* or *trust-building activities* into a search engine yields thousands of sites that provide descriptions of activities and even questions to use in debriefing.

Since the initiative task concept is very broad, it can be used in the classroom, on the school grounds, or off-site. Some of the most powerful initiative task activities take place at camp facilities that can provide the space and apparatus needed to house a permanent setup of equipment and activity stations.

Resident Outdoor Education

A recurring theme of this book is that schooling should reinforce classroom learning by including experiences that provide rich exposure to environments and locations that pull at every sense. Probably the greatest change of pace and place occurs when students leave the school grounds and spend several days and nights in a completely different venue. A resident camp experience provides an extraordinary opportunity to build on schoolyard-enhanced learning experiences while immersing students in a setting that provides a rare disconnect from electronic gadgets and climate-controlled environments.

The Experience

On a warm spring evening in early May, our students had been at camp for three days and were taking part in a "sensitivity stroll," or night hike. My little group of ten sixth graders and I began our hike just as the sun was setting. The kids were animated as they jostled down the trail enthusiastically talking about the experiences of the day.

We came to a large, grassy area and formed a circle. Everyone faced outward, walked twenty paces straight ahead and then stretched out on the grass and looked up at the sky. By now the first stars were faintly visible and it was unmistakable that darkness was fast approaching. Although we were all relatively close together in the field, each of us seemed oddly alone as we lay on our backs looking up at the emerging stars. After awhile, my high school student counselor and I gathered the group back. By now it was totally dark. Interestingly, the ten kids who just a few minutes ago were romping down the path, were now clustered very close to me. A few even held onto my jacket and wanted to take my hand as we walked. It struck me that many of them had never experienced darkness without a light switch or flashlight close at hand.

To lighten up the tone, I pulled out an old camp standby—wintergreen Lifesavers. When you crunch a wintergreen Lifesaver in the darkness (with your mouth open, of course!), it's possible to see flashes of light. This cool phenomenon immediately brings *oohs* and *ahs*, and everyone wants to give it a try.

After we ran out of Lifesavers, we walked slowly to a pine grove near the edge of the field. Once inside the pines, we sat in a tight circle. Everyone then laid back on the pine needle floor and listened to the rich sounds of the night—a thousand chirps and flutters all underscored by the wonderful sound of a gentle breeze moving through the pine boughs.

As I lit a candle, we all experienced a jarring transition. The darkness now seemed so much deeper and almost ominous as we peered beyond the candle's glow. We passed the candle and all were invited to share something that we had enjoyed during the week at camp. The experience was magical—kids were truly expressing deep thoughts and powerful feelings. They talked about making new friends, seeing their teachers in new ways, and seeing "book learning" literally come to life. Some even quietly shared how they conquered initial feelings of homesickness and now had new confidence in themselves.

After sharing, we blew out the candle and let our eyes adjust as we became one with the darkness once again. We then walked quietly back to the main lodge, bound together by an amazing experience that many will remember into adulthood.

You just can't replicate that experience anywhere else—neither indoors nor on the school grounds. Although some schools substitute multiple day trips to parks for resident camping, it's impossible to duplicate the all-encompassing adventure of a multiple-night retreat. The night hike brought reflections and feelings to the surface. But, it was the multiple days of living at the camp that provided involvement and uninterrupted focus on the natural world, nurturing new awareness and forming indelible experiences in the lives of these children.

The resident camp is a classroom with no walls, the sky for a ceiling, and the natural landscape as an audio-visual tool. Living and learning become beautifully intertwined, and students are engaged in the learning process for all of their waking hours. I continue to be amazed at the former students I meet who immediately recall specific learnings, emotions, and experiences that they had during a resident outdoor-education program.

Grade Range and Time of Year

Resident outdoor education can happen at any grade level. Most programs, however, occur at the middle grades (5–8), with grades five and six being the most popular. Resident experiences vary greatly in length, usually ranging from one to four nights. The two-night, three-day format seems to be most popular and provides adequate time for a group to experience a sense of community. Some schools have had success with overnight programs for students as young as third or fourth grade, although these programs usually span no more than one night.

Districts with several K–6 or K–5 schools may use a camp experience in the spring of the final year at the elementary school to give kids a chance to meet students from the other buildings and smooth the transition to the new school. My own introduction to outdoor education came through this type of multischool camping program. Some of the staff and administration from the receiving school helped with the camp so students had a chance to meet some of their future teachers. It's interesting to note that this program is now into its fourth decade of operation and is still credited as a major factor in smoothly combining classes from four different schools to form a new class at the middle school. Kids are comfortable entering the new school in the fall because they have already met the other students in their class, as well as many of the staff.

The time of year does not seem to be a critical factor. For transitional programs like the one just described, obviously, the spring is an ideal choice. However, for programs that are not intended to transition groups from one school to another, the season of the year is not really important. For every person who argues that fall is the ideal time to do a camp, there is another person who is convinced that spring is the perfect season. A fall camp can be an effective way to capture student interest at the beginning of a school year. A spring camp, however, can build upon a variety of learnings that have taken place during the year. Snow and cold do not have to be deterrents. Although the logistical challenges may be a bit greater, the winter season can provide powerful outdoor learning opportunities that most people have never experienced.

Organizing a Resident Program

Outdoor education in a resident setting provides both breadth and depth for teaching a wide variety of content areas, social issues, and interpersonal skills. A good resident program, however, must be carefully meshed with the school's curriculum and should clearly take advantage of unique features available at the camp.

For example, one school utilizes a camp that has prepared an archeological dig site at the former location of an old farmhouse. Kids learn about archeologists and some of the procedures they use, and then actually go to marked quadrants and begin to sift through the dirt. Although they aren't finding treasure, you might think so from the excited shouts of kids who have just unearthed a piece of pottery or a wheel from a child's toy. Without any prompting, kids speculate about how the objects may have been used, where they came from, and how they reflect the era during which the house stood. Social studies concepts become very real when you are literally sifting through history!

Camps usually have natural features that are not available on the school grounds. Ponds, streams, marshes, and acres of mature woods can provide both venue and content for outdoor teaching. One sixth-grade camp program uses the pond as a backdrop for teaching measurement concepts, data gathering, data interpretation, plant and animal classification, habitat studies and even creative writing (from a frog's point of view!).

Although school camp experiences most frequently take place in fall or late spring, I have seen highly effective programs in every month of the school year. The time of year really doesn't matter. What separates an effective integrated program from a detached "week away from school" is careful planning that clearly aligns camp experiences with grade-level content expectations. A well-constructed resident outdoor education program pays careful attention to three major components: precamp, the on-site experience, and post-camp.

Precamp Experience

During this time, give students background information related to the activities that they will be doing at camp. If pond and stream life are going to be explored extensively at camp, then precamp should focus on the terminology, concepts, and processes that are related to aquatic study.

It's a waste of time and resources to do at camp what could just as easily be done at school. Unfortunately, I have too often seen teachers struggle to present lectures complete with worksheets and overheads in a camp dining hall when a regular classroom would have been far more appropriate and better equipped.

On-Site Experience

This is the main event. Many resident programs divide the instructional day into three main parts:

1) Major instructional groups: These are basic "core classes" that every student takes. They may include traditional nature study topics such as birds or pond life; or, broader topics may be included such as problem solving or habitats in nature.

2) Student-choice interest groups: These are usually small-group sessions of ten to fifteen students. The groups meet for a brief time (usually no more than an hour) and students can select the groups that they wish to attend. Topics are extremely varied and offerings may include archery, weaving, pioneer games, geocaching, candle making, and so on. These small interest groups are a great way to involve community members with special hobbies or skills as well as staff members who are not able to take part in the full-day program.

3) Evening programs: The classic evening program is the campfire, probably one of the most impressive and memorable parts of

any camp experience. Night hikes (or, as my school called them "sensitivity strolls") can also provide insights and impression about the outdoors at night that are completely foreign to mos students. Some schools have used GPS equipment to design whole-camp treasure hunts. Another district works with a loca astronomy club to set up telescopes.

Post-Camp Experience

The post camp experience is often the most neglected aspect o resident outdoor education. When the camp experience is completed, i is important to bring the experience back, full circle, to its relationship to the school-based curriculum. A well-planned post-camp curriculum builds on observations, experiences, and data that that were encountered at camp. Writing assignments, math activities, or literature explorations related to camp experiences all help to tie the resident experience to the curriculum. For example, if a school explored an old cemetery near the camp that was the resting place of Civil War veterans, it would be a great post-camp experience to read the novels *Rifles for Watie*, *Shades of Gray*, or another good Civil War title.

Two Approaches to Resident Outdoor Education

School camping takes place in one of two ways—either school facilitated or camp facilitated. In the school-facilitated model, a school staff plans and implements the entire resident-camp experience on its own. Although a camp is rented for the experience, very few, if any, camp staff are utilized in the programming. The school determines its own curriculum, schedule, staffing, student groupings, and logistical needs. The camp usually provides food service, but the school is completely in charge of all other aspects of the camp program.

The school-facilitated model gives the school complete control. The downside, however, is that it takes *huge* amounts of staff time to plan, organize, and finally implement even a relatively brief three-day program. Staff "burnout" can be a real possibility, especially if teachers are on twenty-four-hour duty while at camp.

In a camp-facilitated model, the camp provides trained staff to do much of the instruction and possibly even student overnight supervision. Camps usually provide a list of curriculum options from which the school can choose, and visiting teachers are expected to direct and coordinate some activities during the camp experience.

The camp facilitated model requires far less school time in planning and logistical coordination. Most of the time-consuming details are handled by the camp. The camp staff also knows the land laboratory well and can maximize its usage. Of course, since teachers are not actively involved in planning the program, they may not feel a sense of ownership in the experience and sometimes feel and respond more like visitors than teachers.

Choosing an Approach

Either a camp- or school-facilitated approach to resident outdoor education can provide a highly effective learning experience. As schools decide which approach to use, several factors need to be weighed.

Commitment to Planning

The staff desire to develop its own, unique program is the "enthusiasm" factor, which is the most critical element in the list. Having worked with many school-facilitated resident programs, I am convinced that there must be a core group of staff members who truly feel passionate about developing a camp experience for their students. Notice that I said *passionate*—not just *interested, willing,* or *intrigued.* Unless there are two or three staff who truly feel moved to develop a program from scratch, it might be best to consider a camp-facilitated model.

Staff Time

Staff time certainly relates to the program factor just mentioned. The initial planning for a school-facilitated program takes a lot of time—period! Teachers and administrators need to be willing to devote significant hours outside of the regular workday to plan lessons, locate materials, and develop the schedules, forms, and other needed administrative details. Like any new initiative, the first year of a program is the most complex. In subsequent years, there is far less creation of new material and more emphasis upon revision.

Previous Experience

An extensive background in camping or nature lore is not really that important. Since most resident programs are based at camps with cabins or dormitory-style accommodations, there is little need for teachers to be wilderness survival experts. More important, staff members should share a genuine appreciation for the outdoors and view nature as an opportunity for enriching instruction. Just as you don't need to be a naturalist to use the schoolyard as a teaching tool, you don't have to know every plant and animal to participate in a resident program.

Nearby Camps

From a practical standpoint, camps within a reasonable driving distance can be a major factor. It's just more convenient to use a facility that is less than an hour's drive away. Transportation costs are less and staff can readily check out a nearby camp in advance and set up materials and equipment. Parents also are often more comfortable sending a child to a nearby facility with a familiar name rather than to an unknown place several hours away.

Cost

Cost is influenced by many factors. Length of stay, of course, is a major cost determiner. The use of options such as ropes courses or camp-provided overnight cabin supervision also can impact per-student cost. In most cases, a camp-facilitated program that provides instructional staff will cost more than a school-facilitated program of the same number of days. Of course, if staff planning time for a school-facilitated program is factored in and given a dollar value, the difference may not be very great.

Volunteers

For a school-facilitated program, availability of reliable parents or high school counselors is crucial. High school student counselors can be a wonderful addition to a resident program, serving as great role models for young campers, as well as enthusiastic aides to teachers. It is absolutely essential, however, that these counselors be well trained about the nature and needs of the camper age group, as well as their role in the general instructional program. If you are considering a school-facilitated program, check with your high school early in the process to determine if students can be excused to help with the program. Parents can also be a great resource. A willing pool of parent volunteers also can help to locate resources, assemble teaching equipment, as well as share outdoor-related hobbies and vocations in special interest group sessions.

Leaders

Probably the most important factor in the success of a school camping program is the willingness of someone to take a strong leadership role in the process. Whether the choice is school-facilitated or camp-facilitated camp, there needs to be a key person at the building who is willing to field the questions, do the background research, and, most important, act as a cheerleader for the concept. Most every successful resident camping program that I have seen, whether school- or camp-facilitated, is usually associated with a staff member's name. That person doesn't do it all, but he is definitely the force that motivates others to stay involved.

Why Bother?

Is it a lot of work to put together a school camping program? Absolutely!

Is it worth the effort? Absolutely!

The residential outdoor experience provides tremendous focus and allure. Living in a completely different environment for a few days, without video or technological distractions, naturally makes experiences more vivid and impressions longer lasting. Unfortunately, many children today simply do not view the outdoors as a leisure time option. In fact, many students are, at first, a bit shocked to find that camp cabins do not have TVs or video games. Very soon, however, students become so immersed in exploring where they are that any longing for video vegetation quickly disappears. The realization that there is life without TV or phones is for many students one of the most profound learning experiences that camp provides.

Living together as a group for several days also makes abstract concepts such as consideration, acceptance, and responsibility come alive. The powerful change of pace and place that a resident

The Opportunity for Unique Experiences

Veteran sixth-grade teacher and avid outdoor educator Sue Cook says that she is more convinced than ever that outdoor learning works. Recalling a resident-camp experience, she tells the story of a night hike that included an "owl prowl," an activity where students have to be perfectly quiet as a leader tries to get owls to respond to simulated calls. At best, it's a tricky activity to pull off. If you are lucky, you may hear a few distant responses. However, since kids have a difficult time staying really quiet, the night hike usually moves on after a few minutes of calling and listening.

On this particular night, however, things were different. A distant owl not only responded, but students heard the calls coming closer. As the amazed sixth graders looked up, the owl flew directly overhead, treating the group to a sight that most humans will never see in the wild. The experience truly defined a sense of wonder for Sue's students. As she puts it, "It's impossible to duplicate that on TV!"

Do these experiences have a long-term impact on kids? Sue tells of a former student, now a park ranger on the East Coast, who regularly sends her a donation of 1,000 dollars per year to subsidize costs for kids who might find it difficult, financially, to take part. Now that's tangible evidence of impact!

147

program provides frees both learners and teachers to explore interact, and respond in ways that are not possible in the traditional classroom setting.

The camp experience provides a unique opportunity for students to see teachers differently. The casual dress and tone of the camp environment helps students to see adults as real people rather than just authority figures. Mealtimes, walks to and from field locations and evening activities provide many opportunities for students to have positive interactions with peers and adults. Casual conversations with a favorite teacher after dinner or the sudden feeling of awe and wonder generated by gazing into a night sky filled with innumerable specks of light are memorable moments. Such moments help young and old alike to focus on who they are and what is really important. Because resident camping is a huge change of pace and place for students, the experiences that occur have powerful and long-lasting impact.

Rick Wormeli, a middle school author, lecturer, and practitioner, eloquently describes the impact that resident camping has had upon him as a teacher:

> These are the times when I feel most alive as a teacher and am able to do what middle school students want most from adults: listen, coach, share challenges, demonstrate and applaud strong character, take them seriously, and embrace their potential. Each time I venture forth, I discover additional proof that learning doesn't have to happen in a classroom. (2001, 152)

In Summary

I like the expression "prime the pump." The *American Heritage Dictionary of Idioms* defines it as encouraging the growth or action of something. This is indeed my pump-priming chapter! Although I want to promote the use of the school grounds for teaching, I also want to plant some ideas that will encourage using resources beyond the school. I frequently find that teachers who start taking their classes outdoors regularly are hungry for ways to build on those engaging schoolyard experiences and want to include locales in the community.

This chapter presents quite a mix of ideas! Some, such as GPS activities and initiative tasks, can be done either on the school grounds or off-site. Other topics, including resident outdoor education and hiking strategies, definitely require trips to other locations. My hope

148

is that one or more of these topics will sound intriguing enough to encourage you to explore the ideas a little further. The "Resources" section at the end of the book contains additional references and information about the topics in this chapter.

Postscript

This book has been written with two major purposes in mind. The first is to make a convincing case for viewing the schoolyard as an extension of the classroom. The idea that a classroom can take many forms, and even have the sky for a ceiling and the natural landscape as an audio-visual tool, is empowering. Since the outdoors can provide either a place to teach or content to explore, the schoolyard can be an option for every subject area and grade level. I hope that you will examine your curriculum and see where the schoolyard might provide meaningful enhancements.

I have to admit that the second purpose for writing this book is personal as well as professional. I'm a grandpa now, and that makes me focus a generation ahead. Truthfully, I'm very concerned about the long-term implications of what some authors have called the "denaturing" of society. If adults have had little contact with nature, there will be no impetus to advocate for its protection.

Perhaps by taking kids outside at school, we might be able to occasionally spark that sense of wonder and feeling of "Wow!" I'm quietly hoping that if we take kids outside to do math, someone just might have a butterfly land nearby, or spot a cool-looking insect on a twig. Perhaps that descriptive writing activity on the lawn may go

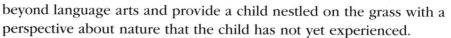

beyond language arts and provide a child nestled on the grass with a perspective about nature that the child has not yet experienced.

But for you to be an advocate for the outdoors, it's important that you frequently experience its beauty, complexity, and ability to soothe, revitalize, and even heal. It's my prayer that you will put this book down, go outside, and enthusiastically immerse yourself in the beauty of creation.

Treat yourself to a change of pace and place!

Appendix A

Directions:

Check with your teacher before examining any plant.
Use your senses of sight, smell, and touch.
Describe, sketch, circle, and comment.
Do not examine roots unless there at least twenty of the same plants in the immediate area.

Plant location _____

_____

Student name _____

Date _____

If It Has FLOWERS:

A. Are there insects on or in the flowers?

_____ Kind? _____

_____

B. Is there one flower or several? _____

_____

C. Where are the flowers located? _____

_____

D. What is the flower color(s)?_____

_____

E. How many petals do you count? _____

_____

F. Describe or sketch the flower shape _____

_____

G. Does it have an odor? _____

H. Can you find unopened flowers (buds)?_____

_____

I. Can you find seeds?_____

1. How do you think the seeds are spread?

   Wind, stick to animals, fall, birds, float.

Sketch, Trace, or Make a Rub Print of a LEAF

153

A. What is the shape? (spear, heart, triangle, long, etc.?)

_____

B. What is the color of the leaf?

_____

1. Are both sides the same? _____

_____

2. Are other leaves the same?_____

_____

C. Do you see what might be insect damage?

1. What is it like? (little holes, edge gone, strange growth, etc.?) _____

2. Can you find anything eating the leaves?

_____

D. How does the leaf edge look and feel? (straight, wavy, toothed, etc.?) _____

_____

E. How does the leaf surface feel? (smooth, rough, fuzzy, etc.?) _____

Are both sides the same?_____

F. Crush and tear a leaf. How would you describe it? (tender, tough, stringy, etc.?) _____

_____

1. Is the inside milky, juicy, sticky? _____

_____

2. Does it have an odor? _____

_____

What Is the STALK(S) Like?

A. How tall is it? _____

B. What color is it? _____

C. Is its shape round, square, triangle, oval?

_____

D. Can you find insect damage? (galls, holes?)

_____

E. If it is a common weed, break and describe.
(hard, soft, hollow, solid, pithy, stringy, etc.?)

_____

If It Is a Common Weed, Pull or Dig It Up to Examine the ROOTS

A. Could you pull it out? _____

1. Did you get all the root?_____

_____

2. Did much dirt stick to it? _____

_____

B. Is there a main root or lots of small roots?

_____

1. Do any large roots run along the ground?

_____

Habitat

A. Is it in the sun or shade? _____

_____

B. Is the soil usually wet or dry? _____

_____

C. Is the soil hard or soft? _____

_____

D. What is the soil color?_____

_____

E. Was it by itself or in a group of its kind? _____

_____

F. Is the soil thickly or thinly covered with plants?

_____

G. Did you recognize any plants growing next to it?

_____

Source: unknown

ur Top Bid	Items for Our Community	Amount Paid
_____	wide-screen plasma TV for each home	_____
_____	many beautiful shade trees	_____
_____	minivan for every family	_____
_____	large community pool	_____
_____	twenty-screen movie theater	_____
_____	large park	_____
_____	good library	_____
_____	giant fast-food court	_____
_____	clear lake and streams	_____
_____	playing fields for sports	_____
_____	forest of big, old trees	_____
_____	nature center	_____
_____	hiking and biking paths	_____
_____	large shopping mall	_____
_____	large golf course	_____
_____	new housing development	_____

155

After your balloon lands, place the hoop over the balloon and look carefully at the area inside the hoop.

First Landing

Type of location: for example, lawn, tall weeds, dirt, and so on.

How many different types of plants can you count? _____

Sketch the shapes of the plants.

What kinds of animals are inside your sampling area?

Second Landing

Type of location: for example, lawn, tall weeds, dirt, and so on.

How many different types of plants can you count? _____

Sketch the shapes of the plants.

What kinds of animals are inside your sampling area?

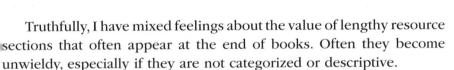

Resources

Truthfully, I have mixed feelings about the value of lengthy resource sections that often appear at the end of books. Often they become unwieldy, especially if they are not categorized or descriptive.

My objective with this section is to provide only a few examples of materials that I have found to be very useful. Since titles are not always self-explanatory, I have annotated the resources so that you can decide if you want to take a closer look. As you explore these resources, please keep the following in mind:

- I have emphasized practicality. Since most readers of this book are classroom teachers, the emphasis is on including resources that directly translate into promoting and implementing schoolyard-enhanced learning.

- This is by no means a comprehensive listing of available resources related to the use of the outdoors for teaching. Although I include a few favorites from my own experience, I'm sure that there are dozens more that could be added under each heading. If you have a resource that you have found to be outstanding, please let me know about it!

- Websites can be extremely useful starting points for exploring a topic. All of the sites here contain links to other sites and resources. Explore sites thoroughly—often great stuff is hidden several layers deep! As we all know, websites come and go My apologies in advance if any of them have moved or been discontinued.

- Complete bibliographic information for books and articles is located in the References section.

More Background Information

Books and Articles

Last Child in the Woods: Saving Our Children from Nature-Deficit Disorder **by Richard Louv**

This book is a must-read for anyone who needs to convince a colleague, administrator, or parent about the value of going outside. Although the book is not written specifically for educators, it is an inspiring work that focuses on the increasing lack of emphasis upon outdoor experience that is so prevalent in society today.

Place-Based Education: Connecting Classrooms and Communities **by David Sobel**

This excellent book is a defining work in the place-based education literature. Sobel not only explains place-based learning, but also provides wonderful examples of how the community can become the focal point for instruction. The book makes an elegant case for grounding learning first in the local and the familiar, rather than in the faraway and abstract.

"Place-Based Education: Learning to Be Where We Are" by Gregory Smith

This frequently cited article provides an overview of the place-based learning concept. Smith also includes several excellent examples of how place-based education can be implemented in schools. If you are looking for a brief overview to give to someone, this may be very helpful.

Websites and Organizations

Wilderdom (http://www.wilderdom.com)

This is an amazingly detailed website created by James Thomas

Neill. The site covers a wide range of topics, some of which include experiential learning, outdoor education, adventure education, and group dynamics. The site is especially useful to those interested in adventure or challenge education. If you visit this site, be sure to take some time to explore several of the links and subpages that are there. The amount of information here is staggering.

Place-based Education Evaluation Collaborative (PEEC) http://www.peecworks.org

PEEC is a partnership of organizations and projects that is interested in evaluating the impact of place based education. If you are looking for research data that explores the value of going beyond the four walls of the classroom, this is the place to begin.

Environment-Based Education: Creating High Performance Schools and Students http://www.neetf.org/pubs/NEETF8400.pdf

This is a publication of the National Environmental Education and Training Foundation (NEETF). On its website, the organization describes itself as

> *Chartered by Congress in 1990, The National Environmental Education & Training Foundation (NEETF) is a private, nonprofit organization dedicated to advancing environmental education in its many forms.*

This report describes a collection of case studies from across the country that document the effectiveness of environment-based education. The studies

> *document current evidence supporting the premise that, compared to traditional educational approaches, environmental-based education improves academic performance across the curriculum.*

This document can provide very useful data and rationale for convincing those who may be skeptical that the use of the outdoors can have an impact on instruction.

State Education and Environment Roundtable (SEER) http://www.seer.org/

The SEER site provides a good review of studies that have been done to analyze the impact of using the environment as a learning context.

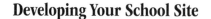

Developing Your School Site

Guides and Articles

Best Managment Practices: Planning First to Make Your Outdoor Classroom Last by the Georgia Wildlife Federation

This very practical and concise planning guide for creating outdoor teaching areas is generously provided as a free download (http://www. gwf.org/resources/wildlifehabitats/bmpindex.html). Brief chapters cover planning, gaining support, site development, maintenance, implementation, and evaluation of school site learning. This guide is an excellent starting point for anyone who is contemplating outdoor learning enhancements.

Plants for Play: A Plant Selection Guide for Children's Outdoor Environments by Robin Moore

This is a very practical resource that provides detailed information about plantings for outdoor play areas. Moore's introduction gives an excellent rationale for the role of plants in play. The book then details very specifically what species of plants are especially useful for play value, seasonal interest, shade quality, screens, and so on. This book is a must if you want to incorporate a variety of plantings on your school site that will promote interest and learning.

"Discouraging Vandalism in Your School Habitat" by Beth Stout

I found this article on the 4-H Wildlife Stewards website (http://www.4hwildlifestewards.org/project%20management/vandalism.htm). It is one of the best overviews that I have found about the very real problem of vandalism that may occur after an outdoor learning site has been created. The article provides some very specific suggestions for making the schoolyard somewhat vandal resistant.

Programs and Initiatives

Boston Schoolyard Initiative

This innovative program began in 1995 and is a wonderful example of a public/private collaborative to enhance schoolyards (http://www. schoolyards.org/home.htm). The publications that can be accessed through the home page provide an overview of the Boston initiative and also provide excellent examples of schoolyard enhancement and rationale for going outdoors.

National Wildlife Federation's (NWF) Schoolyard Habitats Program

The NWF has a program that encourages schools to use the schoolyard as a site for hands-on learning. From the website (http://www.nwf.org/schoolyard/index.cfm) you can access the "Happenin' Habitats" page that provides a variety of tips for establishing wildlife habitats on the school grounds. There also are many practical suggestions for working with children outdoors as well as a teacher resources center that provides links to useful articles and websites relating to outdoor teaching.

From this site you can also access a page titled "Field Trips and Safety Considerations." This two-page document provides very practical tips and serves as a great checklist before going outside.

161

School Gardens

Websites

Elementary School Garden Information: The University of California Cooperative Extension-San Diego—http://commserv.ucdavis.edu/CESanDiego/Schlgrdn/HomePage.html

This site provides very practical information for the teacher who is interested in exploring school gardening. It contains basic tips for getting started, planting, maintenance, and suggested teaching activities. I like the fact that the site gives a good overview of important considerations without going into lengthy detail. This is a good starting point for those who are just beginning to explore school gardening. The "resource links" section is especially helpful and has many excellent general references mixed in with the California-specific links.

National Gardening Association—http://www.garden.org/home

The National Gardening Association (NGA), founded in 1973, defines itself as "a nonprofit leader in plant-based education." Linked from the NGA home page is a wonderful school and teacher resource website called "Kidsgardening." From this page, you can access a wide variety of projects and activities related to the gardening theme. You can even sample activities from *Math in the Garden*, a collection of lessons for ages five to thirteen based on the national mathematics standards. This site is a must for anyone interested in establishing a school garden plot (http://www.kidsgardening.com/).

Texas Agricultural Extension Service—http://aggie-horticulture. tamu.edu/kindergarden/Child/school/sgintro.htm

If you are looking for a brief overview of basic planning considerations to keep in mind as you plan a school garden, take a look at this site. It is very user friendly and provides concise overviews of many important considerations that are a part of planning a school garden. The site even has an excellent slide show that describes the planning process in detail.

Lady Bird Johnson Wildflower Center—http://www.wildflower.org/

The native plant database that is accessible at this site is amazing. You can select your state or province and then locate native plants in your area according to light requirements, soil moisture needs, general appearance of the plant, bloom characteristics including color and time of bloom, and so on. It's amazing! This site is a very useful tool if you are interested in including native plants on your site.

Content-Area Outdoor Activities

Guides and Books

"Reaching High Academic Standards on the Schoolyard"—available through the National Wildlife Federation's "Schoolyard Habitats" site

Linking outdoor teaching to academic content standards is critical in today's schools. This brief document can be downloaded at: http://happeninhabitats.pwnet.org/pdf/Academic_Standards.pdf. It shows how schoolyard habitat projects have direct linkages to content standards established by national scholarly organizations in the major content areas. Examples of standards and their linkages to schoolyard habitat activities are provided for mathematics, science, social studies/ geography, English/language arts, and technology. In each content area, examples are provided for elementary, middle, and high school levels. If you need to convince someone that outdoor learning is linked to standards, this is a great place to begin!

Project Learning Tree (PLT) and Project WILD

Both PLT and WILD are extensive resource and activity guides useful in all content areas. Although the material is centered around a "tree" theme (PLT) or a wildlife theme (WILD), the resource books present dozens of activities to teach interdisciplinary concepts across the curriculum and through all grade levels. The activities are even coded to denote which would be especially effective outdoors. Both resource books emphasize the use of activities to teach concepts that are already a part of the curriculum.

The books are usually distributed free, or at minimal cost, to teachers attending one-day training workshops, with the costs often assumed by state natural resource agencies. By contacting the sites following, you can determine whether one or both of these programs is available in your state. Most states have facilitators for both PLT and WILD and offer workshops regularly. The books are excellent and the training is worthwhile!

Project Learning Tree website: http://www.plt.org
Project Wild website: http://www.projectwild.org

Please note that, although I have highlighted PLT and WILD, there are many other excellent programs that provide theme-focused materials that encourage an understanding and appreciation of the environment. A few other examples include:

Project WET: http://www.projectwet.org
Project Food, Land and People: http://www.foodlandpeople.org/
The Leopold Education Project: http://www.lep.org

The National Audubon Society

Audubon has a wide range of educational materials (http://www.audubon.org/educate/aa). The Audubon Adventures environmental education program is designed for grades 3–6 and provides resource kits including student nature news magazines and classroom resource and activity information. The kits are multidisciplinary, focusing primarily on science, mathematics, and the language arts.

Audubon also developed the "First Field Guides" series for ages eight and older. Finding easy-to-use field guides for children can be a challenge, but these guides are designed with kids in mind. There are twelve books in the series. The complete listing can be found at http://www.audubon.org/market/licensed/childrensbooks.html.

Green Teacher

According to its website (http://www.greenteacher.com):

Green Teacher is a non-profit organization which publishes resources to help educators, both inside and outside of schools, to promote global and environmental awareness among young people from elementary through high school. The organization's primary activity is the publication of Green Teacher, *a quarterly magazine full of teaching ideas from successful "green" educators. Each issue of* Green Teacher *offers perspectives on the role of education in creating a sustainable future, practical cross-curricular activities for various grade levels, and reviews of the latest teaching resources. (*Green Teacher *2007)*

The *Green Teacher* magazine is excellent, filled with article primarily written by practitioners who provide specific activitie and teaching techniques. The organization also publishes severa outstanding books, including *Greening School Grounds: Creating Habitats for Learning.* The "Teaching Green" series also has individua books describing teaching activities for the elementary, middle, and high school levels. Their website provides the opportunity to view the table of contents of each publication—a real help when deciding whether to purchase a book.

Mapmaking with Children: Sense of Place Education for the Elementary Years by David Sobel

Sobel emphasizes the importance of children learning mapmaking with a focus on a sense of place—the places where children live and play. Children develop maps of their surroundings and then gradually build upon those experiences to create maps on a larger scale. The schoolyard and community are very much a part of this wonderfu approach to geography education. Sobel sees mapmaking as a multidisciplinary activity that has relevance for teachers of science mathematics, and language arts, as well as social studies.

Articles and Websites

"Archaeology in the Classroom"

This excellent article by Chris Sandlund is available at http://www

digonsite.com/grownups/using.html. It is actually a part of the website for *Dig: The Archaeology Magazine for Kids*: http://digonsite.com/.

"Classroom Pets: Things to Think About" by Sheryl L. Dickstein

This brief article on the ASPCA website at http://www.aspca.org/site/PageServer?pagename=edu_resources_classroompets raises many important questions to consider when exploring the idea of bringing a pet into the classroom. The web page also includes an "Animals in the Classroom" link that has several additional links related to the topic.

United States Geological Survey (USGS)—GPS information—http://education.usgs.gov/common/lessons/gps.html

If you are interested in learning more about GPS devices and their application to education in a variety of content areas, this site provides an abundance of links. The site also includes several excellent links to geocache teaching ideas.

165

Initiative Task References

Books and Websites

Teamwork and Teamplay by Jim Cain and Barry Jolliff

If you are interested in including a variety of initiative task experiences in your teaching, this book is a must! Cain and Jolliff have written one of the most comprehensive books on the subject, including information about rationale, supporting literature and research, processing and debriefing suggestions, instructions for making initiative task equipment, *plus* more than 150 pages of activities.

The Wilderdom.com teambuilding section—http://wilderdom.com/teambuilding/

This is a section of the extensive Wilderdom.com website. It provides background information about the team-building process and also has good descriptions of some team-building activities. Be sure to explore the many links on the page. The resources that unfold are amazing!

Connecting Your Schoolyard to the World: Online Research Collaboratives

The Internet provides an opportunity for schools to expand their exploration of the outdoors well beyond the local community. Terms such as *online student collaboration* and *student scientist partnerships* describe activities in which classrooms can take part in research and data collection that can take place on a national and even international scale.

Several online projects are available that give students an opportunity to do local data collection, data entry, and comparison of information with other participants from around the nation, region, or world. Although the examples given here are large projects, check with local nature centers to see if they have ongoing monitoring programs in which schools can participate. Local universities will also frequently conduct environmental monitoring programs that can involve local schools.

Online research collaboratives give students the feeling of participating in a real scientific study. Students can readily comprehend the importance of accurate data collection, background research, and careful reporting of results. Data collection projects also generate meaningful numbers for plotting, mapping, and graphing activities. The international scope of many online collaborative research projects also provides excellent opportunities to develop map reading skills and greater geographic awareness.

Here are a few examples of online research and/or data collection projects that provide opportunities for students to link with a larger audience. Much of the descriptive information comes from the project websites. Project FeederWatch, The Globe Program, and Journey North are complex programs that provide multiple opportunities for student learning.

Space limitations preclude in-depth descriptions of each project. I apologize in advance for the brief overviews of these very robust projects, but the Web addresses provide links to complete background information and participation instructions. I encourage you to go to the websites and read full descriptions of these programs if the concept sounds like it might be of interest to you and your students.

Organizations and Websites

Project FeederWatch—http://www.birds.cornell.edu/pfw/index. html

Project FeederWatch is a winter-long survey of birds that visit feeders at backyards, nature centers, community areas, and other locales in North America. FeederWatchers periodically count the highest numbers of each species they see at their feeders from November through early April. FeederWatch helps scientists track broad scale movements of winter bird populations and long-term trends in bird distribution and abundance.

Project FeederWatch is operated by the Cornell Lab of Ornithology in partnership with the National Audubon Society, Bird Studies Canada, and Canadian Nature Federation. (http://www.birds.cornell.edu/pfw/Overview/whatispfw.htm)

Local data is combined with data from hundreds of other sites to produce an abundance of distribution maps, trend graphs, and charts. Since data is being collected from observations of bird feeders, not field observations, it is relatively simple for a classroom to participate.

One fifth-grade teacher who has been participating in FeederWatch for more than a decade uses a feeder conveniently located near a classroom window as the data collection site. Students learn to identify common species; they also gain practical experience in scientific data collection. As students enter their data into the international database, they have a sense of being a part of a large scientific study. The main website aggregates the data and builds reports that show such things as bird summaries by state or province, rare birds, trend graphs, and maps showing the winter distributions of birds.

Journey North—http://www.learner.org/jnorth/orientation/ Overview.html

Journey North is an independent organization, established with a grant from the Annenberg Foundation and supported by Annenberg Media.

This is a multifaceted program that uses seasonal change as a major organizer. Such phenomena as length of day, the appearance of flowers, or the flight of a butterfly are used as the focal points for data collection and research experiences. The Journey North site gives an

167

overview of these three major, seasonal change activities that school
can utilize:

*Sunlight and the Seasons: Children study seasonal change in sunlight in a
global game of hide and seek called Mystery Class.*

*Plants and the Seasons: Children explore tulip growth in their own gardens,
running an experiment that tracks the arrival of spring.*

*Seasonal Migrations: Children follow animal migrations. They observe,
research, and report findings and watch journeys progress on live maps.*

All three exploration topics are excellent. The tulip-growth activity
is especially unique in that it gets students outside planting bulbs in
the fall and then again in the spring as they watch for the emergence
of the plants. Data is logged into the site and the progression of spring
in North America is dramatically visible.

Monarch Watch —http://www.monarchwatch.org/index.html

A related site—Monarch Watch—also focuses on this amazing
butterfly. Based at the University of Kansas, Monarch Watch provides
a place for children to showcase their research or school projects. The
site also provides an opportunity for classes to become involved with
monarch research projects, including tagging.

The Globe Program —http://www.globe.gov/fsl/html/aboutglobe.
cgi?intro&lang=en&nav=1

The GLOBE website gives this overview of the program:

*GLOBE is an interagency program funded by the National Aeronautics and Space
Administration (NASA) and the National Science Foundation (NSF), supported
by the U.S. Department of State, and implemented through a cooperative
agreement between NASA, the University Corporation for Atmospheric Research
(UCAR) in Boulder, Colorado and Colorado State University in Fort Collins,
Colorado.*

*GLOBE (Global Learning and Observations to Benefit the Environment) is a
worldwide hands-on, primary and secondary school-based education and
science program.*

For Students, GLOBE provides the opportunity to learn by:
- *Taking scientifically valid measurements in the fields of atmosphere, hydrology, soils, and land cover/phenology—depending upon their local curricula*
- *Reporting their data through the Internet*
- *Publishing their research projects based on GLOBE data and protocols*
- *Creating maps and graphs on the free interactive Web site to analyze data sets*
- *Collaborating with scientists and other GLOBE students around the world*

GLOBE is truly international in scope with 35,000 teachers participating from 109 countries. To participate in GLOBE fully, teachers need to be trained in professional development workshops that are offered worldwide.

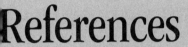

References

Adkins, Carol, and Bora Simmons. 2003. "Outdoor, Experiential, and Environmental Education: Converging or Diverging Approaches?" *ERICDIGESTS.org*. http://www.ericdigests.org/2003-2/outdoor.html.

Albright, Mary Ann. 2006. "Kids Dig into Archaeology." *Corvallis (OR) Gazette-Times*, July 19. http://www.gazettetimes.com/articles/2006/07/19/news/community/a1wed02.txt.

Armitage, Kevin. 2007. Personal communication, May 29.

Bender, Sheila. "Writing Poetry from Personal Experience." *Recreate.com*. http://www.recreate.com/Pages/articles/sbender.shtml.

The Boston Schoolyard Initiative. 2001. "Designing Schoolyards and Building Community." *Boston Schoolyard Initiative*. http://www.schoolyards.org/text/Schoolyard.pdf.

———. 2005. *Grounds for Celebration and Hope, 1995–2005: A Decade of Transforming Boston Schoolyards*. Report to the Mayor, Boston, MA: Boston Schoolyard Initiative.

Bourne, Barbara, ed. 2000. *Taking Inquiry Outdoors: Reading, Writing, and Science Beyond the Classroom Walls.* Portland, ME: Stenhouse.

Cain, Jim, and Barry Jolliff. 1998. *Teamwork and Teamplay.* Dubuque IA: Kendall/Hunt.

Campbell, Bruce. 2005. "The Naturalist Intelligence." *New Horizons for Learning.* http://www.newhorizons.org/strategies/mi/campbell.htm.

Carson, Rachel. 1965. *The Sense of Wonder.* New York: Harper and Row.

Cornell, Joseph B. 1979. *Sharing Nature with Children.* Nevada City, CA: Ananda.

Duffin, Michael, Amy Powers, George Tremblay, and PEER Associates. 2004. *Report on Cross-Program Research and Other Program Evaluation Activities 2003–2004 .* Cross-Program Research Report, Concord, NH: Place-Based Education Evaluation Collaborative (PEEC).

Gardner, Howard. 1993. *Frames of Mind: The Theory of Multiple Intelligences.* New York: Basic Books.

Georgia Wildlife Federation. 2005. "Best Management Practices: Planning First to Make Your Outdoor Classsroom Last." *Georgia Wildlife Federation/Programs/Wildlife Habitats.* http://www.gwf.org/resources/wildlifehabitats/bmpindex.html.

Green Teacher. 2007. "Green Teacher: Who We Are." http://www.greenteacher.com/whoweare.html.

Kaplan, Stephen. 1995. "The Restorative Benefits of Nature: Toward an Integrative Framework." *Journal of Environmental Psychology,* September: 169–182.

Knapp, Clifford E. 1992. *Lasting Lessons: A Teacher's Guide to Reflecting on Experience.* Charleston, WV: ERIC Clearinghouse on Rural Education and Small Schools.

Lamb, Gregory. 2005. "We Swim in an Ocean of Media." *Christian Science Monitor*, September 28: 13.

LaRoche, Donna. 2006. "Lesson Plans—-Geography of Pizza." *National Geographic*. http://www.nationalgeographic.com/ xpeditions/lessons/03/g35/pizza.html.

Lieberman, Gerald A., and Linda L. Hoody. 1998. *Closing the Achievement Gap: Using the Environment as an Integrating Context for Learning*. San Diego, CA: State Education and Environment Roundtable.

Louv, Richard. 2005. *Last Child in the Woods: Saving Our Children From Nature-Deficit Disorder*. Chapel Hill, NC: Algonquin Books of Chapel Hill.

Marzano, Robert J. 2003. *What Works in Schools: Translating Research into Action*. Alexandria, VA: Association for Supervision and Curriculum Development.

Monkman, Drew. 2001. "Sun Shelters: Respite from the Rays." In *Greening School Grounds: Creating Habitats for Learning*, by Tim Grant and Gail Littlejohn, eds., 86. Gabriola Island, BC: New Society Publishers and Green Teacher (copublishers).

Moore, Robin C. 1993. *Plants for Play: A Plant Selection Guide for Children's Outdoor Environments*. Berkeley, CA: MIG Communications.

National Council for the Social Studies. 2004. *Curriculum Standards for Social Studies: II. Thematic Strands*. http://www.socialstudies. org/standards/strands/.

National Council of Teachers of Mathematics. 2000. *Principles and Standards for School Mathematics*. Reston, VA: National Council of Teachers of Mathematics.

173

National Environmental Education and Training Foundation. 2000
"Environment-Based Education: Creating High Performance Schools
and Students." *National Environmental Education Foundation,*
September. http://www.neefusa.org/pubs/NEETF8400.pdf.

National Research Council. 1996. *National Science Education
Standards.* Washington, DC: National Academies Press.

National Wildlife Federation. 2004. "Field Trips and Safety Tips." NWF
Schoolyard Habitats website. http://happeninhabitats.pwnet.org/
pdf/Field_Trip_Tips.pdf.

———. 2007. "Schoolyard Habitats Native Plants Fact Sheet." *National
Wildlife Federation—Outside in Nature.* http://www.nwf.org/
outside/pdfs/nativeplants.pdf.

Neill, James. "What Is Outdoor Education? Definitions." http://www.
wilderdom.com/definitions/definitions.html.

Paul, Richard, and A. J. A Binker, eds. 1990. *Critical Thinking: What
Every Person Needs to Know to Survive in a Rapidly Changing
World.* Rohnert Park, CA: Center for Critical Thinking and Moral
Critique.

Phillips, Autumn. 2003. "Elementary Students Learn About Critter
Control." *Steamboat Pilot and Today,* February 7. http://www.
steamboatpilot.com/news/2003/feb/07/elementary_students_
learn/.

Place-Based Education Evaluation Collaborative. 2006. "Place-based
education and student achievement." *Place-Based Education
Evaluation Collaborative.* http://www.peecworks.org.

Powers, Amy L. 2004. "An Evaluation of Four Place-Based Education
Programs." *The Journal of Environmental Education* V, (4): 17–32.

Schiff, Paul. 1996. *Twenty/Twenty: Projects and Activities for Wild
School Sites.* Columbus, OH: Ohio Department of Natural Resources,
Division of Wildlife.

Sharp, Lloyd B. 1943. "Outside the Classroom." *The Educational Forum*: 361–368.

Smith, Gregory A. 2002. "Place-Based Education: Learning to Be Where We Are." *Phi Delta Kappan*, April: 584–95.

Smith, Julian, Reynold Carlson, Hugh B. Masters, and George W. Donaldson. 1970. *Outdoor Education,* 2nd ed.. Englewood Cliffs, NJ: Prentice-Hall.

Sobel, David. 1998. *Mapmaking with Children: Sense of Place Education for the Elementary Years.* Portsmouth, NH: Heinemann.

———. 2004. *Place-Based Education: Connecting Classrooms and Communities.* Great Barrington, MA: The Orion Society.

State Education and Environment Roundtable. 2006. "EIC-related research." *State Education and Environment Roundtable.* http://www.seer.org.

———. 2006. *The EIC Model.* http://www.seer.org.

Stokes, David W. 1986. *Reaching for Connections, Vol. 1.* Milwaukee, WI: Schlitz Audubon Center.

Texas Cooperative Extension Service. *Theme, Concept and Topic Gardens.* http://aggie-horticulture.tamu.edu/kinder/theme.html.

United Nations Educational, Scientific, and Cultural Organization. 1975. UNESCO/Education: "The Belgrade Charter." http://portal. unesco.org/education/en/file_download.php/47f146a292d047189 d9b3ea7651a2b98The+Belgrade+Charter.pdf.

University of California Cooperative Extension Service–San Diego. Elementary School Gardens. http://cesandiego.ucdavis.edu/ School_Gardens/.http://commserv.ucdavis.edu/CESanDiego/ Schlgrdn/HomePage.html.

175

Vanhoozier, Amanda. "Theme, Concept and Topic Gardens." Aggie Horticulture Network. Texas Cooperative Extension. http:// aggiehorticulture.tamu.edu/kinder/theme.html.

Van Matre, Steve. 1974. *Acclimatizing: A Personal and Reflective Approach to a Natural Relationship.* Martinsville, IN: American Camping Association.

Wormeli, Rick. 2001. *Meet Me in the Middle.* Portland, ME: Stenhouse.

Index

179

181